Integrated Outdoor Education and Adventure Programs

Stuart J. Schleien
Leo H. McAvoy
Gregory J. Lais
John E. Rynders

SAGAMORE PUBLISHING
Champaign, IL

Production Manager: Susan M. McKinney
Cover design: Michelle R. Dressen
Editor: Jana Waite
Copyeditor: Phyllis L. Bannon

Library of Congress Catalog Card Number:92-60846
ISBN: 0-915611-59-7

Printed in the United States.

We dedicate this book to Jason David Schleien, who was born and died during the development of this book. He is greatly missed by his family and friends. We also dedicate it to all children who continue to provide us with the inspiration to facilitate social integration of individuals of varying abilities.

&

CONTENTS

Appendices

ACKNOWLEDGMENTS

We would like to express our appreciation to a number of individuals and agencies who participated in the research and development of this book. We are grateful for their commitment to integrated outdoor programs, their dedication to quality research and programming, and their generous cooperation in sharing their extensive knowledge and experience.

The contributions of a number of graduate students in the Division of Recreation, Park, and Leisure Studies at the University of Minnesota were very important in the outdoor education research and program development aspects of this book. Many of the concepts in this book have evolved from a unique and fruitful partnership between the University of Minnesota and Wilderness Inquiry. We want to especially thank those students for their commitment and exemplary work. These students include Lynn Anderson, Julie Feller, Tammy Freimund, Rick Green, Jeanine Gregoire, Linda Heyne, Debra Hornfeldt, Jean Larson, Cheryl Light-Shriner, Dan Ramier, Molly Schlaefer, Janice Storms, Allison Stringer, Mary Stutz, and Douglas Wahlstrom. We especially acknowledge the contributions of Cheryl Baldwin, Kathy James, Beverly Hawkins, Char Shaffer, and Jeannie Weis in curriculum development portions of the book.

The staff and participants of Wilderness Inquiry have generously shared their knowledge and experiences to provide many of the high adventure components of this book. The integrated adventure program photographs and illustrations in the book were provided by Wilderness Inquiry. Wilderness Inquiry staff who have provided significant input to the book include: Kelly Cain, Holly Church, Howard Cohen, Deb Erdmann, Tracy Fredin, Wayne Freimund, Al Gustaveson, Jay Johnson, Jeanne Kogl, Ione Lindquist, Jane Link, Becky Lucas, Craig Luedemann, Suzanne Mades, Don Mitchell, Robin Monahan, Tim O'Connell, Carol Perry, Kevin Proescholdt, Paul Schurke, Bill Simpson, Patti Thurber, and William Waring.

We would like to give special thanks to staff at the outdoor education centers and agencies who participated in our various research and demonstration projects, especially the staff at Belwin Outdoor Education Laboratory-St. Paul Public Schools, Dowling Urban Environmental Education Center-Minneapolis Public Schools, Lowry and Richardson Nature Centers of Hennepin County Parks, Wilder Forest Outdoor Education Center, and Wood Lake Nature Center. Many of the outdoor education program photographs in the book illustrate programs at these centers. These centers and staff members have provided programming assistance and a commitment to integrated outdoor education, and we appreciate their efforts.

To all the participants in our research and demonstration programs, thank you. We were able to learn and grow from your participation.

We especially would like to thank Joyce Burt for her diligent and outstanding work in preparing the book manuscript, and Sylvia Rosen for her careful editing of our work.

Most importantly, we wish to express our appreciation to all the key players who had the courage and foresight to move beyond the traditional approaches to outdoor education and adventure program service delivery. The creativity of consumers, care providers, professionals, volunteers, advocacy agencies, students at the University of Minnesota, and staff of Wilderness Inquiry has enabled persons with and without disabilities to benefit from each other's presence in outdoor education and adventure opportunities.

PREFACE

It is a common belief that happiness depends on one's leisure. In *Ethics*, Aristotle wrote, "...we occupy ourselves so that we may have leisure, just as we make war in order that we may live at peace." British novelist G.K. Chesterton believed that "leisure was the opportunity for personal and idiosyncratic pursuits, and not for ordered recreation. Above all, free time was to remain free of the encumbrance of convention, free of the need for busyness." In a similar vein, yet relating specifically to outdoor education, William Woodsworth, teacher, scholar, and lover of everything natural, stated, "Come forth into the light of things. Let nature be your teacher." And the noted naturalist and conservationist, John Muir, stated the rationale for outdoor education when he said, "I live only to entice people to look at nature's loveliness."

If we take these poetic words to heart, there is something very important about studying a snowflake, observing the behaviors of pond inhabitants, or learning how to cross-country ski. These activities are but a sampling of outdoor education available to children in elementary schools, to teens exploring their neighborhoods, and to adults seeking new, rewarding leisure skills. But planning creative and enjoyable uses of discretionary time is a challenge for people with disabilities, and consequently, these natural pursuits become even more compelling.

Outdoor education is a discipline in which participants develop an appreciation and understanding of nature and a recognition that such an understanding contributes to the quality of life. It is education in, about, and for the outdoors. It may be a process, a place, a purpose, or a topic. For example, as a process, outdoor education can focus on school subjects by using resources typically found in nature. Students can be required to measure the length and depth of a stream to develop math, motor, and social skills, as well as to acquire scientific knowledge. Socially integrated outdoor programs and activities are enjoyed in schools, parks, natural resource agencies, camps, wilderness areas, adaptive recreation departments, social service agencies, one's backyard, and many other environments. Outdoor education methods and activities include a wide array of approaches that fit the seasons and they are sponsored by a variety of agencies.

Generally speaking, the holistic purpose of outdoor education is to foster a lifelong appreciation of the outdoors and wilderness. In this way, outdoor education fosters stewardship of our natural resources. This attention to stewardship of the earth is especially important in these times of heightened awareness of the importance of taking care of the environment. Humans have the ability to cause significant damage to the natural environment. Everyone involved in outdoor education has the responsibility to help create an environmentally literate and aware population and to offer guidance in ways that everyone can act responsibly regarding the natural world. As an extension of an individual's habilitation or individualized education program, integrated outdoor education promotes positive changes in behavior, emotional adjustment, self-esteem, physical development, socialization, and friendship among people of varying abilities.

Outdoor education is a potent force in accomplishing these goals because it offers a stimulating learning environment. With a low human population density, low levels of noise and movement, and a slow rate of change, the outdoors presents a high level of predictability. Additionally, teachers, therapists, therapeutic recreation specialists, volunteers, and family members can interact with participants in non-school and non-work environments. By focusing on the participants' strengths, outdoor education programmers may discover needs unrecognized in more traditional settings. And participants with and without disabilities learn to trust and depend on each other for comfort and safety in an outdoor setting that is equally novel to both. This very absence of a controlled or contaminated environment permits all participants to discover innovative ways of interacting with and learning from each other as they live, work, eat, explore, discover, and play together. In many respects, an outdoor education or wilderness group is the ultimate team. These settings are naturally conducive to team building, and staff members can do many things to facilitate the process.

Although some programs emphasize individual challenges and activities, the goal of social integration in mixed-ability groups is better served if programs give high priority to group functions. Cooperative groups help equalize everyone's participation, avoiding the "excess baggage syndrome" and the tendency for some to sit passively on the sidelines. A sense of community and teamwork is built by stressing the importance of group functions and accomplishments. What one individual can do is not as important as what the group can accomplish. We all need assistance at times, even staff members, and we should not be afraid to ask for it. But collectively, no challenge can inhibit a group.

Based on these benefits, it should be clear why substantial energy and effort are being directed to outdoor education. Recent state and federal legislation, such as Human Rights Acts (Department of Human Rights, Chapter 363) and the Americans with Disabilities Act (Public Law 101-336), mandate public access in outdoor environments. These laws have helped spearhead and guide programming in municipal, state, regional, and national parks. However, we must go beyond these laws to exploit the full benefits from these programs and settings. People of all ages and abilities are not only becoming active in our camps, YMCAs, Scout troops, 4-H groups, parks, wilderness areas, and outdoor education and nature centers, but they are also learning to enjoy, appreciate, and preserve the outdoors in thoughtful and cooperative ways.

This book presents many ideas, stories, and resources to help you plan exciting, integrated programs in the outdoors. We are certain they will stimulate your imagination and senses and enhance your dreams of the possible.

S.J.S.
L.H.M.

THE AUTHORS...

DR. STUART J. SCHLEIEN is a Professor of Therapeutic Recreation and Director of Graduate Studies in the School of Kinesiology and Leisure Studies at the University of Minnesota. He holds an adjunct appointment in the Department of Educational Psychology-Special Education Programs. His research efforts involve the development of technology to integrate children and adults with developmental disabilities into community leisure environments. Dr. Schleien has written over 60 journal articles and book chapters, and six books. He has presented his work at professional conferences and symposia throughout the United States, and in Canada, Israel, Australia, and Sweden. He is currently the Chairperson of the Leisure and Recreation Committee of The Association for Persons with Severe Handicaps (TASH) and has served on the President's Committee on Mental Retardation. He was recognized by the Arc of Minnesota as the Minnesota Educator of the Year in Mental Retardation and by the Minnesota Recreation and Park Association as the Researcher of the Year in Therapeutic Recreation and Leisure Education.

DR. LEO H. MCAVOY is a Professor of Outdoor Education in the School of Kinesiology and Leisure Studies at the University of Minnesota. He is the Division Head of the Division of Recreation, Park, and Leisure Studies, and holds an adjunct appointment in the College of Natural Resources. His primary areas of research are the development and evaluation of strategies to integrate persons with disabilities into outdoor education and recreation programs and environments, and the management of outdoor education and recreation programs and facilities. Dr. McAvoy has written over 45 journal articles and book chapters, and two books. He has presented 52 papers at national and international scholarly meetings. He is an elected member of the Academy of Leisure Sciences, received the Contribution to the Enhancement of Life for Disabled Individuals award from the Minnesota Occupational Therapy Association, and the Excellence in Environmental Education award from the Minnesota Association for Environmental and Outdoor Education.

MR. GREGORY J. LAIS is the founder and Executive Director of Wilderness Inquiry and has managed the program's growth and development for more than 15 years. He is nationally recognized as one of the pioneers in outdoor recreation programs serving people with disabilities. An expert in design and implementation of integrated outdoor programs, Mr. Lais has developed outdoor policies, written staff training manuals, adapted outdoor curriculum, developed adapted equipment, and published several articles on integrated programming. He has instructed over 75 wilderness canoeing adventures involving persons with physical, cognitive, and emotional disabilities. Under the direction of Mr. Lais, Wilderness Inquiry has received many awards, including the Organization of the Year Award from the National Therapeutic Recreation Society and special recognition from the White House.

DR. JOHN E. RYNDERS is a Professor in the Department of Educational Psychology-Special Education Programs at the University of Minnesota. Licensed as a Special Educator and School Principal, Dr. Rynders taught children with severe disabilities for five years and was a school principal for three years. He has written more than 40 journal articles and book chapters, and four books. He has delivered 37 professional papers at national and international conventions, has been a Fullbright Scholar, received the Meritorious Service Award from the National Down Syndrome Congress, and has been recognized as a Distinguished Alumnus of the University of Wisconsin-Stout. He is a licensed Consulting Psychologist in Minnesota and is called upon frequently to assist parents of children with disabilites to advocate for improved educational programming.

Snowshoe winter ecology program.

Chapter One

A RATIONALE FOR INTEGRATED OUTDOOR EDUCATION AND HIGH ADVENTURE

The winter Ben was in the seventh grade, his mother enrolled him in an integrated program at the local nature center. Its focus was snowshoe instruction and ecology. Although Ben had to struggle with the instruction, the encouragement of the other children helped him persevere. Like the other children, he acquired new skills—putting on snowshoes, walking and turning in the snow, hiking through the woods, and spotting the winter homes of animals. He had more difficulty learning how to step over a log with snowshoes, however. But he refused to give up and finally was able to perform the difficult act. Ben exulted, "I can do it! I can do it!" while the other members of the group cheered. It was a wonderful moment for the group because Ben has Down Syndrome, has mental retardation, and has physical limitations. The participation in a group composed mostly of children without disabilities was a wonderful first for him.

A spinal cord injury left Barbara with paralysis below the waist. She was a professional and competent intellectually; she missed the travel and adventure she used to enjoy. A friend recommended that she go on an integrated wilderness canoe trip. At first it was frightening—she wasn't sure she could learn the skills and keep up with the group. She was also nervous about how the people without disabilities would respond to her. But her fears were groundless. The integration skills of the leaders, the instruction and skill practice sessions, and the camaraderie of the group helped everyone enjoy the beauty of the wilderness and the joy of a successful group experience.

At the last campsite everyone sat around the fire and related their thoughts. Barbara summed up her feelings with some emotion. "I feel normal now," she said, "and I didn't before. I feel positive now about facing new experiences; before I was afraid. If I can do things I never dreamed of in the wilderness, I know I can do them back home too."

Jack, a businessman who likes the wilderness, had no disability. He told of the surprise he felt at the capabilities of the trip participants with disabilities. In his evaluation after the trip he wrote, "I now understand people with disabilities better. Disabled people are no different than others, except for a disability. I learned not to be afraid of them. I am not afraid to approach disabled people. I don't pity them because I know they can do a lot."

These accounts are typical of the experiences of many others, both with and without disabilities. They also illustrate three major movements in educational and leisure arenas spanning the present and coming century:

— Outdoor education,

— High adventure programs, and

— Social integration of people with disabilities.

The momentum for these movements started in the 1970s when the U.S. Congress and the Supreme Court outlawed segregation of people with racial, intellectual, and ability differences. The courts ruled that equal access to programs and environments is a civil right; thus, people with disabilities have the right to life, liberty, and the pursuit of happiness just as do those without disabilities. The result has been greater access to mainstreamed programs and services for persons with disabilities. This right has been reinforced by Congress through the Rehabilitation Act of 1973 (P.L. 93-112), the Education for All Handicapped Children Act (P.L. 94-142), the Architectural Barriers Act (P.L. 90-480), and the Americans with Disabilities Act (P.L. 102-336). These legislative mandates provide a basic framework for integration efforts throughout our schools, communities, and outdoor recreation resources and are part of the movement toward normalization.

Implications of Integrated Community Recreation Participation

The movement toward normalization has increased placement of individuals with disabilities in age-appropriate, regular-attendance public schools, and in smaller, integrated living situations. The Education for the Handicapped Act mandated the right of *all persons* with disabilities to be placed within the *least restrictive environment* (LRE) (*i.e.*, environments that provide the greatest opportunities for an individual to develop intellectually and socially). LRE not only covers school placement but also extends to involvement in community-service activities. Normalization stresses the delivery of services in environments and under circumstances that are as culturally normal as possible. Accordingly, services for people with disabilities should include the broad array of activities available to most residents of a community. The word "all" and the phrase "least restrictive environment" have created unprecedented opportunities to integrate persons with disabilities into regular schools, recreational facilities, and other community settings. Let's look at a few of these opportunities.

1. Integrated programming promotes the development of *functional recreation skills*. The person with a disability who will live in a group home or a supported living setting as an adult should learn how to use the local park, outdoor education center, and other recreational opportunities. Moreover, these community recreation experiences should involve participants who do not have disabilities, because everyone must function in an integrated society.

2. Integrated programming promotes *independent/interdependent functioning*, which is crucial for successful community living. Special education and rehabilitation often emphasize preparing a person with a disability to live independently.

Independence should not be the only goal of outdoor recreation, however, because even few people without disabilities are entirely independent. All of us are part of complex, mutually beneficial, formal and informal, interdependent support systems. A person with a disability needs to learn to become appropriately interdependent, for example, asking a bus driver for assistance. Thus, an integrated outdoor environment should present challenges that result from openness (e.g., integration) rather than the predictability of self-containment.

3. Integrated outdoor programming offers *mutual benefits*, that is, benefits to all participants—with or without disabilities. People sometimes assume that the benefits of integrated activities accrue solely to people with disabilities. This is not true; benefits of sound, integrated programming are at least as great for nondisabled participants in developing self-perception and social sensitivity. There are times in the formative years of an individual without a disability when interaction opportunities with a peer with disabilities fosters an improved capacity for compassion and kindness while enjoying cooperative recreation activities. Interacting successfully with persons who have disabilities helps those without disabilities to view all persons as valuable to society.

Integrated outdoor education and adventure programs benefit everyone—participants with disabilities, peers without disabilities, outdoor education professionals, and administrators. Integration with peers without disabilities lessens the social isolation experienced by many with disabilities and provides more positive role models than "handicapped only" programs. Individuals learn new behaviors by imitating peers. Only exposing individuals with disabilities to others with disabilities lessens opportunities to acquire socially and age-appropriate behaviors.

For many persons with disabilities, most interactions with nondisabled people are instructional and occur in educational settings. But opportunities for non-instructional, social interactions are equally important. Integrated outdoor education and adventure activities provide the ideal environment for development of non-instructional peer friendships. Children without disabilities who grow up with children who are disabled become more aware of similarities rather than differences. They also are more accepting of people with disabilities they meet later on and are more supportive of the basic human rights of all citizens.

Program instruction in integrated settings provides appropriate behavior standards for children with disabilities, given inappropriate behaviors are usually not tolerated by nondisabled peers. For outdoor education professionals, integrated programs eliminate many generalization problems that are incurred in artificial environments. In integrated programs, skill instruction takes place in the setting in which it will be used, eliminating the need to later transfer skills to more natural environments.

In the rest of this chapter we illustrate how these movements in education and community recreation benefit individuals and society. We also develop a rationale for organizations and individuals to support and initiate integrated outdoor education and high adventure programs for persons with and without disabilities.

Definitions and Descriptions

Who are these people with disabilities? They are individuals in our society who have physical and/or developmental disabilities (including mental retardation). The disabilities may range from "mildly disabled" to "severely disabled." However, first and foremost, individuals with disabilities are unique persons with unique personalities.

What is outdoor education? Generally, it is defined as the process by which an individual (a) develops an understanding of the natural environment, (b) learns to appreciate the natural environment, and (c) recognizes that the understanding so gained contributes to our general quality of life (Ford, 1980).

The methods and activities of outdoor education include a wide array of approaches—from the study of the composition of a snowflake (to broaden an understanding of physics), to the observation of animal homes (to gain an understanding of the effects of pollution), to the acquisition of snowshoeing skills (to increase leisure skills and to learn to enjoy winter). Most outdoor education, as the name implies, occurs outdoors, but there are many outdoor education activities that can be accomplished indoors.

Outdoor education activities usually are sponsored by such agencies as schools; municipal, state, regional, or national parks; other natural resource agencies (*e.g.*, wildlife foundations); non-profit organizations (*e.g.*, foundations, camps, and social service agencies); and even some for-profit organizations (*e.g.*, wilderness travel companies).

High adventure programs are organized excursions into a wilderness or semi-wilderness environment. Here, participants are led through a series of activities—sometimes risky—that result in personal growth and fulfillment. The risk may be objective (*e.g.*, whitewater rafting) or emotional (*i.e.*, engaging in new activities and stretching one's perceived limits). These programs have been functioning for decades in the United States.

Integration, whether educational, political, recreational, or social, is both a *goal* and a *process*. The *goal* is to ensure that persons with disabilities are (a) accepted as members of the community, (b) permitted to participate in activities enjoyed by other members of society, and (c) able to participate in the activities alongside peers without disabilities. The *process* of facilitating integration is not an easy one. It requires social as well as physical integration before relationships can be formed that support mutual benefits and outcomes.

The philosophy and technology of integration were developed in such areas as special education and vocational training; they are now applied to community leisure activities, camp programs, and wilderness trip programs.

Goals of Integrated Outdoor Education

Outdoor education has an important holistic purpose: *to develop life-long attitudes, skills, and knowledge to further understanding and appreciation of the world in which we live.* We are stewards of all our natural resources—those that are economically valuable and those that improve the quality and joys of life. For example, if we do not know the kinds of trees and ground cover needed by different species of birds, we may inadvertently destroy their habitats and hence the birds themselves.

Other goals of outdoor education are directed toward people. Outdoor education programs enhance self-esteem, physical development and coordination, positive changes in behavior, emotional adjustment, and the acquisition of social interaction skills and friends. These goals are of equal benefit to persons with and without disabilities.

For persons with disabilities, outdoor education and high adventure environments and programs often have barriers that are difficult to detect. Despite legislation to provide greater physical, programmatic, and educational accessibility to them, barriers still exist. As a result, these facilities and programs are underutilized by persons with disabilities.

Integration is a planned process by which individuals with and without disabilities are involved in mutually beneficial activities. Mutual involvement in an activity facilitates social integration. Social and physical integration differ. *Social integration seeks to develop acceptance and necessary social skills for mutually beneficial relationships between individuals with and without disabilities.*

The integration process focuses on the abilities, interests, and needs of individuals with and without disabilities by creating a broad spectrum of services and opportunities so that each individual may participate in the activities of daily living in a natural environment. Integration provides opportunities to participate in activities appropriate to an individual's age, gender, and other norms and routines of life. As a process, integration requires professionals to become more aware of adaptations of equipment and facilities that promote physical integration and of group facilitation techniques and cooperative teaching strategies for social integration.

People with disabilities often have difficulty in some aspects of daily living, especially in such areas as accepting themselves as worthy of respect and human dignity; interacting with peers in a socially acceptable manner; interacting with authority figures (*e.g.*, parents, teachers, and employers) in a consistently acceptable and productive fashion; and engaging in constructive psychomotor, cognitive, and affective learning activities without frustration, conflict, and failure. One way that outdoor education helps ameliorate these problems is by opening a stimulating learning environment that offers a high degree of predictability.

This kind of environment has a low population density, low levels of noise and movement, and a slow rate of change.

Benefits of Integrated Outdoor Education

People benefit from exposure to nature—being outdoors—whether it is at a city park, the seashore, mountains, or a primitive area. Just being there, breathing the air, is exhilarating—but there can be more. That is where outdoor education comes in: it not only teaches people how to enjoy nature, but it also enlarges their lives, both cognitively and affectively. Unfortunately, much of the outdoor education and environmental education literature concerning participants with disabilities has focused on segregated programs, that is, programs directed at selected disability groups. McAvoy & Schleien (1988), however, expanded these studies to integrated groups (*i.e.*, groups made up of persons with and without disabilities). A number of benefits accrue to participants in such groups, including cognitive gains in environmental concepts, increased levels of social interaction between persons with and without disabilities, increased peer acceptance, a decrease in socially inappropriate behaviors, and an increase in learning life-long outdoor leisure skills.

The courts have ruled that public schools must have an individualized educational plan (IEP) for every child with a disability. Outdoor education is an extension and a broadening of this principle. Integrated outdoor education:

1. Facilitates learning by enabling individuals to apply abstract concepts learned in classrooms to nature.

2. Provides opportunities for learners to develop group-learning, social, and self-care skills under supervision.

3. Provides family members, teachers, aides, volunteers, paraprofessionals, therapeutic recreation specialists, and recreation professionals with opportunities to interact with participants in non-school, non-work environments, and to assess and identify strengths and abilities masked by their disabilities.

4. Provides opportunities for students to grow in self-esteem and pride in their accomplishments.

5. Facilitates socialization among peers with and without disabilities and encourages individuals to learn to trust and depend on each other for comfort and safety.

6. Places all participants who are unskilled in an outdoor activity on an equal footing.

7. Provides acceptable adult and peer role models whose behavior individuals can imitate.

8. Provides an environment where participants with disabilities can discover and learn new ways of interacting with others.

Most benefits are gained by participants, but family, teachers, and therapists also profit. The potential for every participant to benefit personally, socially, emotionally, cognitively, and physically is great. Outdoor education programs make it possible for every participant to achieve some success in physical and creative efforts and in relationships with new people.

High Adventure Programs

Friends at a campsite in the Northwest Territories.

Many people dream of high adventure—climbing the Alps, canoeing swift rivers, or exploring unknown territories. Modern adventure organizations have made such dreams come true for many (*e.g.*, African safaris). Over the past decade, some organizations have extended high adventure programs to persons with disabilities, integrating them with persons without disabilities. In addition to outdoor high adventure, these programs provide opportunities for people with and without disabilities to participate in experiences that encourage peer relationships as well as inspiring personal development—personal growth, self-confidence, and awareness of the natural environment. These experiences inspire all participants to maximize their vocational, educational, and leisure potentials.

An underlying goal of integrated high adventure programs is to provide positive experiences for everyone in the group in settings that empower them to expand perceived limitations. In these outdoor adventures, participants are provided with opportunities:

— To experience social integration in settings far removed from the everyday environment;

— To increase self-esteem and self-confidence;

— To promote independent living skills for persons with disabilities;

— For persons without disabilities to look beyond disabilities and to discard negative stereotypes; and

— To recognize similarities between people with and without disabilities.

With time and experience, organizations informally determined that integrated wilderness programs provide beneficial experiences for all participants. A recent study (McAvoy *et al.*, 1989) documented that integrated high adventure programs result in positive attitude and lifestyle changes for participants. They interviewed 40 participants, both with and without disabilities, after completing a seven - to 12-day wilderness trip sponsored by Wilderness Inquiry, Inc., a Minneapolis-based nonprofit organization. The positive changes included attitudes toward persons of varying abilities, interpersonal relationships, confidence levels, willingness to take risks, feelings about self, goal-setting abilities, leisure skills, tolerance of stress, and in 36 percent of the participants with disabilities, increased ability to live independently.

In summary, the rationale for integrated outdoor education and adventure programs is a complex matrix of legal, educational, social, and psychological reasons, including:

1. *Individuals with disabilities learn social skills necessary for mainstreamed life.* Persons with disabilities need peer models. When they are separated from peers without disabilities, they only have other people with disabilities or adult care providers from whom to learn and practice appropriate social behavior. Furthermore, classroom experience is not enough. The "street wisdom" learned in uncontrived, real-life situations and the nuances of social interactions with peers are not easily taught or learned. Outdoor education and adventure environments are places where people socialize as well as learn. With the richness of opportunities in these environments, individuals with and without disabilities learn social and natural interdependence.

   Such interactions usually sensitize people without disabilities to the abilities of those who are disabled, and they help overcome personal fears and develop adaptive communication skills necessary for positive relationships. Peers without disabilities learn greater acceptance of "differentness." Apparent individual differences become less of a stumbling block to personal involvement and social interactions. Continual exposure to and interaction with persons with disabilities help dispel stereotypes of what individuals with disabilities can or cannot do or be.

2. *Individuals have the opportunity to make meaningful contributions and build self-esteem.* Individuals need to feel that they can contribute to situations and activities and will be recognized for those contributions, whatever the setting. The challenges and learning opportunities in outdoor education

and adventure environments are intrinsically valuable to people, whatever their abilities. Positive feelings developed through participation in these programs help individuals define or change the picture of themselves and their capabilities. Approximately 60 percent of all individuals with disabilities are unemployed, but outdoor education experiences may help them overcome feelings of inadequacy and build self-confidence. Unfortunately, many educational, vocational, and recreational activities still segregate people by physical or cognitive ability. We need programs that integrate people into the physical, social, and economic mainstream of society. Integrated outdoor education and adventure programs provide opportunities for challenging experiences and for persons with physical disabilities to meet in value-free surroundings with people without disabilities. Instead of segregating people according to perceived abilities, integrated programs include all people as peers.

3. *Integrated programs are cost-effective.* The most frequent reason voiced by public administrators for not providing integrated, accessible programs is the exorbitant cost. Yet when we consider the cost of building, maintaining, and staffing separate, "handicapped" facilities, trails, and programs versus the cost and long-term benefits of providing integrated, accessible facilities, the choice is clear—integrating existing programs is cost-effective.

   The handicapped "blind" trails established during the 1970s provide a good example of the then-prevailing solution for accessibility. After a period of infrequent use and high maintenance, administrators and staff discovered that people with visual impairments preferred the "regular" trails that emphasized their similarities to peers without disabilities.

4. *Integrated programs are critical to a high quality of life.* Learning about, understanding, and appreciating the natural world around us are primary goals of outdoor education. This interaction with nature offers us peace of mind, beauty, and wonder. We cannot deny such a relationship to persons with disabilities. When asked, "Why integration?" consider what it would be like if we were able to go only to "handicapped events," or to use only "handicapped facilities," or to associ-

ate only with other "handicapped friends." *Quality of life* is correlated with diversity and choices. Persons with disabilities often are limited in their choices due to inaccessible facilities and programs, discriminating attitudes, isolation from the mainstream, and few opportunities to socialize with people who are not disabled.

After a rainy day on the trail.

The following list of curricular domains for integrated outdoor education and adventure programs is organized according to skills that can be acquired by participants with and without disabilities.

1. Psychomotor, physical, and skill development.

   a. Learn to function efficiently and effectively in outdoor environments.
   b. Improve overall physical abilities.
   c. Improve physical fitness level (*e.g.*, strength, endurance, agility, coordination, and balance).
   d. Acquire life-long leisure skills.
   e. Learn and develop outdoor living skills: travel (*e.g.*, hiking, canoeing, skiing, and biking), campcraft, survival, *etc.*
   f. Improve sensory awareness: respond to stimuli in the environment and to other people and activities.

2. Cognitive abilities.

    a. Learn the relationship of humans to nature.
        — Interdependence with environment.
        — Ecological concerns.
        — Conservation of natural resources.
        — Impact of humans on natural resources.
        — Develop a sense of stewardship for the environment.
        — Examine current issues related to the environment.
    b. Learn about wildlife and plant life.
        — Human effects on and interactions with fauna and flora.
        — Preservation and protection of the resources.
    c. Learn concepts of outdoor living activities.
        — Navigation (*e.g.*, map, compass, and orienteering).
        — Low-impact camping and travel techniques.
        — Selection, use, and care of equipment, clothing, and food.
        — Survival skills.
        — Campcraft skills (*e.g.*, fire use, stove use, and food preparation).
        — Safety procedures and considerations.
    d. Develop an understanding of how to solve problems.
    e. Understand the importance of learning activities that can be engaged in during leisure time.
    f. Understand the values of participating in outdoor activities, including physical, social, and cognitive benefits accruing to individuals and groups.

3. Affective, social, and attitudinal skills.

    a. Increase self-confidence and self-esteem.
    b. Improve group cooperation and interaction skills.
    c. Improve communication skills.
    d. Develop a sense of responsibility.
    e. Learn leadership skills.
    f. Develop self-motivation, self-direction, and sense of independence.
    g. Develop willingness to accept new challenges.
    h. Learn to cope with new or unexpected situations.

i. Test and clarify personal values.
j. Learn to cope with stress.
k. Develop attitude of social responsibility.
l. Develop decision-making abilities.
m. Develop creativity.
n. Develop aesthetic appreciation of nature.
o. Develop positive attitude toward integration of persons with and without disabilities.
p. Develop cooperative living skills with peers.

The list above illustrates a range of benefits. However, all recreation specialists, outdoor education leaders, and other personnel should keep in mind the main reason that persons with disabilities participate in outdoor education and adventure programs. They are not seeking therapeutic benefits. They are looking for the same things that people without disabilities have in mind when signing up for outdoor programs—feelings of accomplishment, developing a connection to nature, making friends, improving skills, overcoming natural obstacles, and testing their limits.

Approximately 38 million Americans have some form of disability. Some segregated programs and facilities serve a minority of persons with disabilities, including "trails for the handicapped," programs for special education classes or residential homes for persons with mental retardation, and one-time programs for a select disability group. Social and financial forces, however, make many segregated programs too isolationist and expensive to staff. Integrated outdoor education and adventure programs offer opportunities for everyone to become aware of and appreciate the natural and cultural resources of the outdoors.

Adventure programming is for everyone.

Chapter Two

ADMINISTRATIVE PROCESSES

When a local outdoor education and camping facility offered a program to increase children's understanding of the role of domestic animals in our culture, a question arose about admitting 13-year-old Jill. She lives in an intermediate care facility for children and young adults with developmental disabilities. Jill uses a wheelchair and requires total assistance for all daily activities. Nonverbal, she is able to express herself through smiles, laughter, eye contact, and crying. She loves being outdoors and with animals.

The prospect of admitting Jill into the outdoor program raised some administrative questions. What kind of transportation would she need? Would an extra staff member or assistant need to be assigned to her? Would specialized equipment be needed to move her around the activity site? Could she have access to the animals? And would there be additional liability for the facility? After several discussions, the questions were resolved and Jill was enrolled in the program.

Needless to say, she was an enthusiastic participant, although the extent of her participation was limited. But the other members of the group were quick to provide help. In the sheep barn, for example, Jill was moved from her wheelchair to sit on the floor with her nondisabled peers. They used hand-over-hand assistance to help her become familiar with the feel of newborn lambs. They devised a participatory role for her in carding wool and making art creatures out of the wool felt. Jill's smile at the end when she sat petting a very young lamb was an unmistakable indication that she had benefitted from the program.

Outdoor education and adventure programs and facilities, like most social and educational services, are embedded in administrative structures. The programs are usually offered by nonprofit or governmental agencies (*e.g.*, schools, park departments, social services, or other service organizations) and are regulated by administrative requirements and exigencies of funding. Many agencies and organizations adhere to rigid planning and management that make changing or offering new opportunities difficult. When confronted with requests to integrate individuals with disabilities into programs and facilities, some organizations insist that, although they support integration as a concept, it is impossible to implement. Such administrative obstacles as facility inaccessibility, lack of trained staff, and other logistical problems are cited. Whether these administrative obstacles exist is not the point, because there may well be obstacles to successful integration, but they are not insurmountable. In this chapter, we discuss strategies that can be successfully employed by staff members of outdoor education and high adventure programs who want to make integration a reality.

The obstacles and recommended strategies are presented in matrix form at the end of the chapter. We urge readers to use it as a convenient reference to identify and eliminate obstacles to integrated programming.

Organizational Goals and Mission Statement

Administrative obstacles cited as reasons for delaying integration of programs and facilities should be considered realistically in terms of organizational goals and the mission statement. If the stated priorities of an agency do not include serving persons with disabilities, spending time and dollars on integrated programs is difficult to justify. But most public and nonprofit human service and education agencies are mandated to offer services to everyone, regardless of ability level. Thus, it is incumbent upon agencies to examine their mission statements and program goals to determine if they reflect the mandate. If not, agencies should develop appropriate goals and rewrite their mission statements to include serving individuals with and without disabilities in integrated programs.

The next step is to examine participant demographics for existing programs. What is the extent of participation by persons with disabilities? Is this population being served by existing programs? Are programs integrated (*i.e.*, do persons with and without disabilities participate together as peers) or segregated (*i.e.*, do persons with disabilities participate in "special" groups)? Segregated programs serve a need as a transition offering (*i.e.*, "stepping stone") to help persons with disabilities move toward participation in integrated activities. However, if all participation is segregated, goals should be established to support integrated programs.

New goals should establish the commitment to integration, that is, to provide opportunities for all participants (both with and without disabilities) to interact physically and socially as peers in the same activity. Once such goals are included in the mission statement, administrators and program planners are on the way to meeting legal obligations and are justified in the use of resources and facilities. Integrated programming need not be expensive or resource consuming; in many cases, it may simply require a broadened awareness and a shift in attitude about what is possible.

Funding and Logistics

The *development* of integrated outdoor education and adventure programs may be costly. Initial costs per participant in an integrated program may be up to 40 percent more than those for traditional programs. Most added expenditures are due to increased staffing, although facility modifications, increased staff time spent on developing programs, staff training, changing promotional literature, needs assessments, making arrangements for transportation for program participants, and additional equipment all add costs. But most of these costs will be significantly reduced after the program is developed. Once programs are established, however, staffing costs can be reduced by using volunteers to work with participants.

Other strategies can be used to solve funding obstacles, including:

1. Incorporate facility accessibility improvements as priority items in capital improvement and maintenance budgets.

2. Seek interagency cooperative funding with community education, parks and recreation, adaptive recreation, special education, and social services. If such funding is not possible, these agencies may be able to provide some staffing or staff training as a contribution.

3. Seek funding and/or grants from local, state, or federal agencies, private foundations, and local service clubs (*e.g.,* Lions and American Legion). Many foundations, corporations, and service clubs give priority to programs serving persons with disabilities.

4. Work with agencies and businesses to fund promotional literature.

5. Request bus transportation for participants; solicit schools, special education funds, or service clubs and businesses for needed transportation.

6. Offer integrated programs at a time and place when parents are available for car pooling.

7. Check with local "handicapped access" transportation services, such as Metro Mobility, and have the outdoor program site included on regular public transportation routes.

8. Borrow adapted equipment from participants' homes and agencies that serve persons with disabilities (*e.g.,* special education classrooms, group homes, and rehabilitative facilities) or have maintenance people modify equipment as necessary.

Safety and Liability

Issues of safety and liability are often primary administrative obstacles to initiating integrated outdoor programs. Fear of participant injury and a resulting devastating lawsuit are concerns given that our society has become very litigious, especially when a potential defendant is an institution, and the injured party is viewed as vulnerable. An integrated programmer has four tasks in relation to safety:

1. To reduce unnecessary risk through adequate training and proper program design.

2. To convince the sponsoring agency that the proposed outdoor program is not unreasonably risky.

3. To convince participants, parents, and care providers that the program is safe.

4. To conduct the program in such a way that the probability of an accident is low.

A number of outdoor program agencies and organizations have produced safety standards for specific activities. The most used set of standards, *Accepted Peer Practices in Adventure Education*, was developed by the Association for Experiential Education (AEE). Recently, AEE published *Safety Practices in Adventure Programming* (Priest & Dixon, 1990), which is a comprehensive discussion of safety and leadership responsibilities as well as specific safety measures for most outdoor adventure activities (*e.g.*, camping, bicycle touring, rock climbing, caving, skiing, kayaking, canoeing, and sailing).

The following general steps can help accomplish the complementary goals of conducting a safe, injury-free program and minimizing the likelihood of liability suits:

Thorough program planning. Devising a well planned, well documented program with accompanying written policies and management procedures is an effective step toward ensuring a safe program. The plan should address all issues affecting the program and participants and should include the following documents:

— Participant permission and registration forms.

— Records of staff qualifications and training.

— Medical information forms.

— Procedures for responding to accidents.

— Records of program and staff evaluations.

Documentation should also include written staff procedures for conducting all activities and for anticipated problems that may arise in each activity. For an example of staff and program procedures in integrated outdoor activities, see Appendix A.

Appropriate numbers of qualified staff members. If an agency cannot provide enough qualified staff, then an integrated outdoor program should not be initiated. Program success depends on the qualifications of the people in charge. "Qualified" means that the staff member has appropriate skills for a particular outdoor activity as well as for working with persons with varying abilities. Each staff member is properly trained in safety precautions for the activity and participant groups. [See Priest & Dixon (1990) for information on credentials for outdoor program leaders.]

It is difficult to set a universal staff-to-participant ratio for all integrated outdoor programs because of the range of programs and participant abilities. However, an effort should be made to achieve "natural proportions," that is, to set a standard similar to the proportions of persons with and without disabilities in society. Sometimes such a standard is not possible or practical, but program planners should establish the participant-to-leader ratio according to the following criteria:

— Type of program or activity.

— Leader abilities and qualifications.

— Environmental conditions where the activity takes place.

— Physical-cognitive requirements of the activity.

— Special needs of participants.

— Safety margins.

Some programs may need a staff member for each participant or one for every two participants, such as a winter camping expedition that integrates teens with and without developmental disabilities or an integrated camping trip that includes patients from a psychiatric hospital with behavior problems. In a one-day (or shorter) integrated outdoor education program that includes children with developmental disabilities, an effective ratio may be three staff members to four children with developmental disabilities and eight children without disabilities. A wilderness canoe program that includes adults with and without physical disabilities may include two staff members, five participants with disabilities (but only one or two with severe mobility restrictions), and five participants without disabilities. By following these examples, appropriate ratios for specific outdoor programs can be developed. Whatever the ratio, wilderness trip groups should be kept to a maximum of 10-12 persons, including staff. When a group exceeds this number, there is less group interaction, less efficient supervision, more chance that a participant may be lost or that needs will not be met, and more human effects on the environment. Specific standards for participant-to-instructor ratios can be found in Priest & Dixon (1990) and by referring to agencies such as Wilderness Inquiry and Outward Bound.

Activity and location appropriate for participants. The judgment of leaders and participants determines how appropriate activities and locations are for individuals. If participants are allowed to engage in activities inconsistent with their abilities and experience, the chance of injury is greatly increased. An assessment of participant skill and ability level is essential; then necessary training and proper supervision must be provided before and during each activity. Program leaders should consult with participants so that they can work out appropriate activities and locations. For example, it may be undesirable to have a participant with severe circulation problems participate in a winter camping trip because of potential injuries arising from sensitivity to cold. But that same person could participate in winter skiing, dog sledding, or hill sliding if overnight accommodations are indoors. Or the same activity opportunities may be provided in a day program without an overnight stay. Examples of training to raise the skill and awareness levels of participants include:

— Offering one-day training workshops near home to give participants of varying abilities the opportunity to try outdoor activities and to develop skills.

— Holding an introductory camping trip on the agency grounds or a nearby park before taking a group into a remote area.

— Practicing canoeing in a swimming pool or at a local beach to see if a participant with a prosthetic device can get out of a swamped canoe.

Pre-trip screening is particularly important on extended wilderness adventure trips. These screenings help ascertain the mobility level and emotional appropriateness of participants. See Chapter 3 for a screening procedure.

Develop a sense of community—an atmosphere of self-responsibility. If a sense of community and identification with the activity group and sponsoring agency can be developed, not only will participants and staff gain more from the experience, but also an injured participant may be less inclined to sue (van der Smissen, 1979). Suits will not be eliminated, but they may be reduced. Developing an atmosphere of self-responsibility for safety both in individuals and in the group can be accomplished to some extent in all populations. Because one program goal should be to teach outdoor leisure skills for use both inside and outside of formal programs, training should be provided in how to safely canoe, bicycle, cross-country ski, ride a horse, fish, camp, hike, swim, or kayak.

The emphasis on self-responsibility also includes impressing upon participants that the staff cannot be everywhere at one time, watching over every person. Participants should be encouraged to be responsible for their own bodies and their own safety. Staff members should emphasize that, because some activities have a potential for injury, all participants should help each other and the staff provide as safe an environment as possible. Safety rules should be established for each activity. Staff members must insist that participants understand and adhere to all safety rules; for example, wearing life jackets in a canoe, wearing helmets when biking or rock climbing, and wearing a hat and sunscreen when spending the day in the sun. Encouraging self-responsibility can relieve staff members from spending most of their time guiding participants around obstacles.

Inform participants of potential risks. A primary defense against a liability suit is referred to as "assumption of risk," that is, the person is fully aware of the risks involved in an activity and decides to participate. If injury occurs, it is more difficult for the person to collect damages because the courts may hold that the person understood the possibilities for injury. For participants to assume risk, however, they must first understand the potential risk for each and every activity. Staff members must work with participants in pre-trip meetings, interviews, and in written and oral communications to ensure that they understand and appreciate the potential risks.

The process of informing participants of risk should be documented, with participants acknowledging in writing that they understand possible risks and agree to follow safety rules. If participants are minors or vulnerable adults, their parents or guardians must sign such acknowledgments. In an institutional setting, the forms often must be signed by medical personnel. If a person has a disability, it is advisable for medical information and risk acknowledgment forms to be signed by a participant's physician, even if the participant is in a community-based living setting or living at home.

Along with informing participants of potential risks, actual participation in each outdoor activity should be on a voluntary basis only. If a participant chooses not to participate, but is forced to do so by staff members and an injury occurs, the probability of a lawsuit is increased. Also, clients who are forced into participation probably will pay little attention to safety rules and will be more likely to be injured than others in the program. (See Appendix B for examples of participant medical forms and "assumption of risk" forms.)

Supervision. Supervision in outdoor programs must be constant to prevent accidents. Such programs often put people in totally new environments where hazards (*e.g.*, weather and rugged terrain) are real and immediate medical assistance is not available. Any mistake in judgment that results in injury is greatly magnified under these conditions. Supervision includes close monitoring of the progress and condition of all participants; it also includes provision of appropriate equipment and constant checking of such equipment as climbing ropes, life jackets, and stoves.

Concern with legal liability is used by some agencies as a reason for not making facilities and programs available to persons with disabilities. However, the legal liability of integrated programs is no greater (and no less) than that incurred with other programs. More information on legal issues in outdoor programs can be found in McAvoy (1982), McAvoy *et al.* (1985), Priest & Dixon (1990), and van der Smissen (1990). Outdoor programs demand that:

— Agencies and staff members must operate facilities that adhere to appropriate standards of safety if they are to be open to children, youth, and adults.

— Facilities must be constructed and maintained according to these standards.

— Equipment must be appropriate for the activity and the participants and be properly maintained.

— Areas unsafe for particular individuals either must be improved or deemed off limits to them.

— Staff members must be trained in appropriate safety techniques and emergency reaction procedures, which are standardized and well documented.

— Staff members must be trained to provide programs appropriate to the skill levels and capabilities of participants under appropriate supervision.

— Staff members must exercise good judgment in using facilities and program components according to the abilities of participants.

All these "musts" are general responsibilities of the staff and agencies to provide safe opportunities for all participants.

Physical Accessibility

Learning about camouflage and animal coloration.

Outdoor education and adventure facilities were seldom designed or constructed initially to provide accessibility for persons with physical or multiple disabilities. Many buildings, trails, teaching stations, and other facilities were built decades ago. In many outdoor adventure areas, it would be inappropriate to undertake the massive grading and alterations necessary to provide wheelchair access to every section of a park, nature reserve, or wilderness area; landscape alterations that endanger natural resources are neither necessary nor desirable. Like other nature lovers, persons with disabilities want aesthetic qualities and wildness maintained. But primary facilities at an outdoor education and high adventure area can be made accessible to persons with disabilities by sensitive and innovative administrators and program planners.

A first step in providing accessibility is to conduct an inventory of facilities to identify (a) levels of accessibility, and (b) where problems exist. Inventory the accessibility of parking areas, walkways, doorways, restrooms, stairs and steps, trails (*i.e.*, surface, grade, and width), campsites, observation sites, and teaching stations. (See Appendix C for a detailed accessibility inventory checklist and set of suggested standards for outdoor education sites.) Accessibility standards for indoor and outdoor facilities are available from state and federal agencies that serve persons with disabilities and can be used to design specifics (*e.g.*, width of doorways and trails to accommodate wheelchairs, acceptable surface and grade for trails, and methods of providing access to water areas). Architectural standards for buildings also are available.

Once problem areas are identified, then steps can be taken to improve facility accessibility. Some modifications may be relatively inexpensive and easily accomplished, such as lowering work tables so they can be reached by persons in wheelchairs, or eliminating a slight change in grade at the start of a floating walkway. Other modifications (*e.g.*, widening doorways, installing ramps for stairs, or providing a nature trail with a hard surface and acceptable grade) are more elaborate and expensive and may have to be phased in. As long as facilities are modified according to accepted construction and design standards, and are properly maintained, the agency need not fear that legal problems will arise from accidents.

However, most outdoor education facilities and high adventure activity areas contain areas that are just not accessible. It is important to document those areas and the problems they present. Advanced program planning is necessary to avoid inaccessible areas.

Participant Recruitment

Persons with disabilities have a history of not participating in outdoor education and adventure programs for a variety of complex reasons. These include inaccessible facilities, exclusion from outdoor programs due to purposeful or benign neglect of organizers, parental overprotection (fear of injury), and lack of opportunity to develop outdoor skills (*e.g.*, camping, canoeing, hiking, or skiing) or a feeling of comfort in the outdoors. Many persons with disabilities have been protected from interacting with the outdoors on even a basic level (Peterson, 1978). They have been kept out of the sun and the rain, kept away from insects and water (lakes, ponds, and streams), and usually confined indoors; their failure to take advantage of outdoor education and recreation areas should not be surprising.

Recruiting participants with disabilities takes a significant effort by the agency. Many with disabilities assume that they are not wanted in outdoor education and adventure programs and that their quest to participate would be fruitless. Consequently, a major marketing effort has to be made, first to let people with disabilities in the community know that integrated outdoor and adventure programs exist, and second, to encourage them to participate.

Most agencies severely underestimate the preparation and skills required to market recreational programs in general and integrated outdoor education and adventure programs in particular. To start with, messages have to be directed to persons with disabilities as well as those without disabilities who would be eager to participate in the programs described. Promotional literature must be particularly inviting to persons with disabilities (and to their families); pictures of people with disabilities engaging in some possible activities must be displayed; and clear messages of nondiscrimination must be featured. In addition, visual materials (slide shows and video tapes) of people with disabilities interacting with nondisabled peers in activities are needed for those who do not trust the literature alone.

Communication networks must then be established. Local groups and agencies serving persons with disabilities should be encouraged to participate in promoting and actually programming outdoor activities. Even more important is the development of a network of integrated groups that will use the facilities on a regular basis to create a "user friendly" image and to promote integrated opportunities as the norm for the outdoor facility and program.

Another aspect of successful marketing is convincing persons without disabilities that the programs are not "for the handicapped." The marketing approach must convince potential participants that these programs are for persons of "varying abilities" and a range of participation options are available. Community-based programs must offer skill training and experiences that appeal to everyone. Advertising a kayak program "for the handicapped" will attract only a small proportion of persons with disabilities and very few persons without disabilities, but an instruction program that includes opportunities for everyone to get into a kayak and receive personal instruction, and assistance if needed, could be attractive to a range of participants. A next step may be to offer an integrated kayak adventure trip to an exciting location, such as the San Juan Islands in the Northwest, the Apostle Islands in Lake Superior, or the Maine coast. Simply offering a kayak trip to a local lake will not be attractive enough to persons with disabilities who are seeking more adventure, nor will it attract those without disabilities.

Staffing, Training, Support, and Volunteers

Currently most outdoor education and adventure program staff members are not prepared to work with persons who have physical and/or cognitive disabilities, which must be considered in planning integrated activities. Appropriate training should be made available to prepare staff members to serve persons with disabilities and to become familiar with integration strategies. Good media for such training are (a) workshops led by integration and/or disability specialists and (b) university-level courses in therapeutic recreation, outdoor education, and/or special education. Local advocacy organizations that provide services to persons with disabilities also can provide training. Program administrators must understand the need for training and allocate the resources necessary to accomplish it. Job descriptions for new staff should be revised to include education and training in serving persons with disabilities in integrated settings.

Even with training, some staff may have negative attitudes toward serving persons with disabilities. Administrators must reinforce the value of integrated programs. All the training and facility modifications will be wasted if staff members are not enthusiastic about or interested in integrated programs. Some practical methods of improving staff member attitudes are:

— Evaluate the interest of staff members and select one interested person to act as coordinator of these new efforts.

— Provide that individual with the training to integrate persons with disabilities, and then empower that person to train other staff members and assist them in gradually integrating other programs.

— Involve staff members in setting integration goals and making accessibility improvements.

Problems with accessibility often are more a matter of attitudes and beliefs than of actual physical problems. The staff may believe that integrated programs are too difficult to conduct because of physical limitations of a site and their uncertainty of how to handle logistical challenges presented by persons with physical disabilities. They may also believe that participation of people with disabilities in a group activity may dilute or compromise the experience for others. How does one get a wheelchair next to a bog to collect samples? How can a person with visual impairments or who is deaf and blind participate in a camping program?

Many negative stereotypes and perceptions can be eliminated by educating staff members in the characteristics of persons with disabilities. A greater understanding can help staff feel comfortable enough with persons with disabilities to ask how they can access certain environments. A trained staff also can anticipate accessibility needs. Staff members who accept the challenge of integrating programs often are able to brainstorm ideas or methods to make programs and facilities more accessible. A number of journals and magazines specialize in adaptive equipment and methods, such as *Adapted Physical Activity Quar-*

terly, Exceptional Parent, Palaestra, Sports and Spokes, and *Therapeutic Recreation Journal.*

Another method of making facilities and programs accessible is to form a network with agencies that serve persons with disabilities. Many such agencies would like to have their clientele integrated into outdoor education and high adventure programs. These service providers include special education teachers, social workers, therapeutic recreation specialists, parents, care providers, and local program leaders for the Association for Retarded Citizens (Arc), the Muscular Dystrophy Association, and others (See Appendix D for a reference list of agencies and associations). They can offer excellent ideas on making outdoor facilities and program areas more accessible to persons with disabilities and how programs can be modified.

Outdoor education and adventure programs are staff-intensive activities. Integrated outdoor programs are even more staff intensive, because they require a higher staff-to-participant ratio and a higher degree of training. Administrators have to determine whether their staffs have the appropriate skill levels necessary to integrate persons with disabilities, whether staff attitudes are conducive to the development of integrated programs, and whether adequate staff time is available to develop new integrated programs.

The staff may already be overextended. There simply may not be time available to develop and implement another new program—especially one that is integrated. Many outdoor education program facilities allocate staff to programs on a 1:15 staff-to-participant ratio. Integrated programs may require a 3:10 staff-to-participant ratio and can vary depending upon the activity and the ability levels of the participants. How does an administrator obtain more staff for these programs and justify the expenditures?

One step is to schedule time for staff to develop and implement the integrated program. Administrators may need to explore the possibility of hiring new part-time or full-time staff and arranging for a therapeutic recreation specialist, with training in integration facilitation (see Chapter 4), to consult with the staff.

Recruit volunteers to develop new programming or to assist staff members in developing and leading integrated programs. These volunteers can attend to many social integration needs of mixed groups by encouraging cooperative activities; they can help individuals who require additional assistance or time to complete a task; and they can help in the logistics of working with persons with mobility challenges. Volunteers can free outdoor leaders to concentrate on instruction and leadership of the integrated program. Volunteers (*e.g.*, parents, siblings, students, or members of disability advocacy groups) must be recruited, trained, and supervised. They are often recruited by outdoor agencies because of their interest and expertise (*e.g.*, bird watching, wildflower identification, whitewater canoeing, or rock climbing). Similar volunteers can be found with an interest and expertise in working with persons with disabilities.

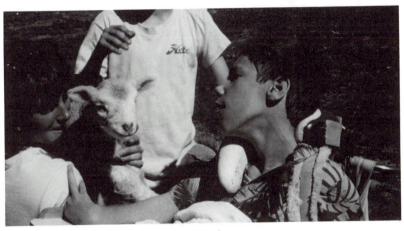

Learning together about domestic animals.

Integration Administrative Concerns Matrix

This chapter has examined administrative components of an integrated outdoor program. The process of bringing components together is often a challenge. The *Integration Administrative Concerns Matrix* (Table 2.1) is designed to help overcome difficulties. It is divided into four major categories that comprise the process of integrating persons with disabilities into the program. Under each category, the process steps, potential problems, and recommended strategies for ameliorating the problems are described.

To begin the process, *Evaluate the Mission Statement and Program Goals* and ascertain who is served by the agency. One may find that the service philosophy excludes persons that challenge the delivery system (*e.g.*, individuals with disabilities). The *Recommended Strategies* column of the matrix offers ideas for rewriting the mission statement and program goals to eliminate discriminatory practices. Then an agency would *Assess Staff Abilities and Availability* for strategies to obtain needed staff, to develop training in integration techniques, and to create staff attitudes conducive to integrated programs. The matrix also describes steps to *Evaluate Financial Feasibility*.

As an agency begins to serve individuals with disabilities, the next section indicates steps to *Examine the Accessibility of Program and Facility to Persons with Disabilities*. If one has grown accustomed to working primarily with nondisabled people, architectural and programmatic accessibility may appear insurmountable. Transporting participants with physical disabilities up steep trails or up a staircase into a nature center must be examined in the planning stages. Practical solutions are given in the matrix. Addressing attitudinal obstacles (*e.g.*, negative attitudes toward persons with disabilities) can pose a greater problem, but steps can be taken to overcome those as well. We hope this matrix will serve as a guide to creative problem solving.

Table 2.1. Integration Administrative Concerns Matrix.

Evaluate the mission statement and program goals

Integration Process	Potential Problems	Recommended Strategies
1. Review mission statement.	Mission statement does not facilitate, or is not conducive to serving individuals of varying abilities.	—Rewrite mission statement to reflect needs of persons with disabilities. For example, it is our mission to provide programs and services that are available and accessible to all persons, regardless of age, sex, religion, socioeconomic status, and level of physical or mental ability. —Educate individuals who write mission statements about the importance of serving all people.
2. Review goals.	Existing goals do not emphasize social interaction and cooperation of all participants.	—Develop goals that include the opportunity for participants of varying abilities to interact to accomplish group goals.
3. Examine characteristics of participants or likely participants (*i.e.*, age, school, drop-in visitors).	Agency has not taken into account all possible participants. Few persons with disabilities participate in programs.	—Survey community for populations and needs, network with disability advocacy groups, obtain accurate information from governmental agencies regarding number and location of residents or market of persons with disabilities.
4. Develop goal implementation.	Agency offers programs for persons with and without disabilities but they are segregated, homogeneous programs serving a particular group (*e.g.*, children who are mentally retarded).	—Brainstorm all opportunities that the agency can provide. —Outline plans to develop integrated heterogeneous programs. —Examine model programs for examples of how others have successfully provided integrated programs. —Network with service agencies for support to include persons with disabilities in integrated programs.

Table 2.1. Integration Administrative Concerns Matrix (continued).

Integration Process	Potential Problems	Recommended Strategies
Assess staff abilities and availability		
1. Evaluate staff attitudes toward integrated programs.	Staff not interested in or enthused about serving persons with disabilities in integrated programs.	—Educate staff on the value of integrated programs and the benefits to participants with and without disabilities.
		—Educate staff on legal mandates to serve persons of varying abilities.
		—Make commitment to integrate programs by scheduling time for staff to concentrate on program planning and implementation.

Table 2.1. Integration Administrative Concerns Matrix (continued).

Integration Process	Potential Problems	Recommended Strategies
Assess staff abilities and availability		
2. Train staff to serve persons with disabilities in integrated programs.	Staff lack skill and experience in working with persons of varying abilities.	—Involve staff in integrated program planning and help identify ways to improve accessibility of the facility and programs along with staff attitudes.
	Staff feel they need to know specifics about all types of disabilities.	—Plan appropriate development sessions: sensitivity training, working with volunteers, and companionship training.
		—Include person with disability at staff meeting where he/she can share personal experiences.
		—Role play to teach skills required to work with integrated groups.
		—Attend workshops on programming for persons with disabilities.
		—Evaluate interest of staff members: select an individual to serve as coordinator of integration training and program development.
		—Hire a consultant to provide training to staff concerning successful integrated programs; this consultant could be a Certified Therapeutic Recreation Specialist (CTRS).

Table 2.1. Integration Administrative Concerns Matrix (continued).

Integration Process	Potential Problems	Recommended Strategies
Evaluate financial feasibility		
1. Determine availability of staff and time for integrated programming.	Staff not available to conduct integrated program.	—Research possibility of hiring additional staff (therapeutic recreation specialist, outdoor educator, special education teacher).
	Lack time needed for preparation of an integrated program.	—Use volunteers, when possible, to assist in facilitation of integrated program.
		—Ensure that scheduling procedures allow for integrated programs.
		—Include in budget possible integration consultant position to train staff (could be a short-term position).
		—Speak with others who have successfully implemented programs to discuss the timing framework.
2. Calculate cost of offering integrated programs.	Funds not available for additional programs, including integrated programs.	—Identify possible funding sources that support services for persons with disabilities (county, state, federal, and private sources).
		—Initiate a "user fee" program to cover costs of integrated program.
		—Examine possibility of support from advocacy groups (*e.g.*, Association for Retarded Citizens).
		—Develop a list of available resources.

Table 2.1. Integration Administrative Concerns Matrix (continued).

Integration Process	Potential Problems	Recommended Strategies
Evaluate financial feasibility		
3. Examine cost of improving facility accessibility.	Funds are not available for facility improvements (*e.g.*, architectural access).	—Incorporate improvements into existing/future capital improvement and maintenance budget.
		—Contact local service groups for possible funding or work projects to make necessary accessibility modification.
4. Develop marketing strategies for integrated programs.	Unable to successfully market integrated program and recruit participants with and without disabilities.	—Coordinate with local service providers to recruit participants with disabilities enrolled in other community programs.
		—Coordinate with school groups, scout troops, and community service agencies to recruit nondisabled participants.
		—Advertise in flyers and newsletters about efforts toward integration; state how programs will be made accessible.
	Parents of children with disabilities believe their child will be left behind or not gain from a program too advanced for their child.	—Explain benefits for all participants to parents.
		—Provide literature to parents describing benefits of integration for all participants.

Table 2.1. Integration Administrative Concerns Matrix (continued).

Integration Process	Potential Problems	Recommended Strategies
Evaluate financial feasibility		
5. Coordinate transportation logistics.	Difficult to transport participants with disabilities to and from integrated program.	—Offer program at a centrally located facility. —Encourage participants to carpool. —Check handicap access programs (*e.g.*, Metro Mobility) for transportation services. —After school program could have school buses drop children off at the program site. —Plan program around available transportation, such as bus schedules or public transportion services. —Lease or purchase a van or bus.

Table 2.1. Integration Administrative Concerns Matrix (continued).

Integration Process	Potential Problems	Recommended Strategies
Examine the accessibility of program and facility to persons with disabilities		
1. Assess and improve facility accessibility.	Doorways, restrooms, and steps are barriers to persons with physical disabilities.	—Implement modifications and improvements of the environment and facility (*e.g.*, build ramps, remove bathroom door and replace with curtain, or conduct program in the most accessible setting).
	Administration believes that extensive changes are difficult at this time.	—Contact state's Handicapped Council on Disabilities or National Accessibility Office: Architectural and Transportation Barriers Compliance Board, Public Information Office, 330 C Street, S.W., Washington, D.C. 20202.
	Outdoor environments are perceived by administration and staff as inaccessible.	—Contact service provider, therapeutic recreation specialist, or special education teacher for activity modification ideas (*e.g.*, using fluorescent paints, improve lighting, enlarge trail signs, or improvise canoe seat).
	Winter activities involving snow appear inaccessible to those with mobility limitations.	—Use sleds and dog sleds to transport those with mobility problems.
	Outdoor program area does not have paved trails and appears inaccessible to those with mobility limitations.	—Leader finds smoothest area possible, slows down the pace for the entire group, and instructs nondisabled peers on carrying techniques to help lift those with disabilities over logs and other difficult terrain.

Table 2.1. Integration Administrative Concerns Matrix (continued).

Integration Process	Potential Problems	Recommended Strategies
Examine the accessibility of program and facility to persons with disabilities		
2: Enhance staff's knowledge of characteristics of disabilities and adaptive equipment ideas.	Staff unfamiliar with characteristics, needs, and abilities of persons with disabilities.	—Conduct staff development sessions on use of adaptive equipment (*e.g.*, sled, adaptive canoe paddles, cooperative learning techniques, and use of trainer advocates/volunteers).
		—Subscribe to professional journals and educational magazines (*e.g.*, *Adaptive Physical Education Quarterly*, *Exceptional Parent*, *Journal of the Association of Persons with Severe Handicaps*, *Palaestra*, *Sports and Spokes*, and *Therapeutic Recreation Journal*) to enhance general knowledge of programming for persons of varying abilities.
	Staff believe integrated program is too difficult to implement.	—Attend conferences, workshops, or extension classes on integrated programs.
		—Contact other agencies that integrate their programs.
	Staff unsure of how to manage logistical concerns.	—Brainstorm with staff to solve problems as they arise.
		—Brainstorm with staff on ways to adapt equipment for participation of all members.
		—Contact careproviders for information on adapting equipment and activities.
	Staff believe person with disability cannot keep up with peers who do not have a disability.	—Educate instructors and leaders on strategies for partial participation, importance of social interactions, attending to task, and providing a stimulating environment for the participant with a disability.

Canoeing the Boundary Waters Canoe Area Wilderness.

Chapter Three

ASSESSING PARTICIPANTS FOR OUTDOOR EDUCATION AND HIGH ADVENTURE ACTIVITIES

George soon realized that he was in over his head. The seven-day integrated canoe trip he is leading looks like it is headed for disaster. For starters, he has four people who use wheelchairs—two of them weigh over 200 pounds each. How was he going to carry them over the trails? One of George's participants has a pressure sore, and another needs an enema every other day. George doesn't know what a pressure sore is, and he doesn't want to learn how to give an enema.

The rest of George's group seem nice, but they don't know what to do. Two members are mentally retarded, and one has Parkinson's disease. To make matters worse, one of the women who uses a wheelchair is strongly opposed to taking "those retarded people" on her trip. She claims their presence is an insult to her intelligence.

George wonders if he will ever make it through this trip. If he does, he intends to have some strong words with the program director who set up this trip.

To determine the quality of activities in an integrated program, an outdoor education professional must be able to assess each participant's needs, abilities, and interests, and match them to appropriate social and physical environments. This process is called assessment. Some simple rules can be applied to significantly increase the quality of assessment. As with any complex task, the key is to break assessment down into its primary components and to tackle each in a sequential fashion. In this chapter, we discuss the components of assessment, provide programmers with general guidelines to follow, and offer hints and examples to make the process more effective.

To start, let's clarify precisely what assessment is—and what it is not. Many think it is a selection process by which people can be excluded from participation in an activity. But in our context it is *a process of matching people's needs with the service capacity of the provider, the demands of the environment, and the needs of other participants to provide high-quality, socially integrated, outdoor activities*. It is a process of seeking the right "fit" between participant needs and quality experiences.

Guidelines for Participant Assessment

Given the importance of assessment to the success of integrated outdoor activities, organizations should develop priorities to use in assessment decisions. Although each agency must develop its own guidelines, the following may be helpful:

Safety. Safety of participants has to be the first priority for integrated outdoor education and high adventure programs. Proper assessment is essential to ensure that each participant's needs can safely be met.

Program quality. Proper assessment is a critical factor of program quality. An imbalanced group can cause significant problems for both staff and participants. Some programs have trouble attracting enough nondisabled participants and conduct their programs with a majority of those who have disabilities. These unbalanced efforts frequently do not result in socially integrated groups.

Social integration. The goal of social integration is best achieved when a mix of persons with diverse abilities is included in the same program. A diverse mix of participants has an increased likelihood for symbiotic relationships, as well as a greater ability to compare and contrast life issues.

Cost-effectiveness. To the delight of program administrators, socially integrated programming can be cost effective. Screening plays a critical role because it establishes:

— Staff-to-participant ratios;

— The ratio of persons who require costly services (*e.g.*, attendants, sign language interpreters, and special transportation) to those who do not; and

— The ratio of persons who require financial assistance to those who do not.

These ratios often determine the financial feasibility of a safe, quality program. Although cost-effectiveness is critical to success, it is not examined in detail in this chapter because of space considerations. Unfortunately, few studies exist on the subject of cost-effectiveness. For more information, we suggest that you contact the agencies listed in Appendix D.

Assessment Factors

The process of assessment is not an exact science. It is difficult to predict whether a program will meet the expectations and needs of every person who enrolls. Careful assessment, however, can minimize placing people in programs that do not meet their needs. Thus, in assessing potential participants, the following factors must be considered:

— The environment;

— The activity;

— The participants; and

— Agency resources.

Although these four factors are discussed separately, they are interactive. Together, they determine what is possible in integrated outdoor programming. Remember that assessment is not an academic exercise—people are being evaluated for admission to programs that could profoundly affect their lives.

The Environment

The environmental setting for outdoor education and adventure is one factor that determines the success of participation of persons with varying needs. Sea kayaking in the Bahamas has an entirely different set of considerations than dog sledding in northern Minnesota. In general, however, outdoor programs take place in areas without roads, pavement, and other conveniences associated with accessibility.

Outdoor education and adventure often incorporate challenges for both individuals and groups. In determining whether a specific environment is appropriate for an applicant, keep in mind the type of challenge desired by both the individual and the group.

Dog sledding— A great way to integrate winter activities.

Basic accessibility. Getting to the terrain where an activity will occur is obviously important, especially for persons with mobility impairments. Long-distance travel through steep or rocky terrain may effectively limit the ability of most users of wheelchairs to participate. Persons who are not mobility impaired, however, may find rugged terrain to their liking.

Remoteness/proximity to help. In very remote areas, the potential for delayed medical assistance must be considered. Some persons may have disabilities that periodically require medical attention (*e.g.*, kidney dialysis). If that cannot be provided on the trail, they may have to be excluded from trips into remote areas. They may be accommodated, however, by outdoor programs in areas closer to developed facilities and medical assistance.

Natural hazards. The potential effects of environmental hazards must be considered when people with disabilities are integrated into outdoor education and high adventure programs. Such hazards include poisonous snakes, extreme cold, and biting insects. Persons with poor circulation and/or those who lack mobility are at a distinct disadvantage in bitterly cold weather. Persons who have reduced use of their arms are at a disadvantage when it comes to fending off mosquitoes and biting flies. In most cases, natural hazards need not specifically exclude persons with disabilities, but they must be considered and adjustments made.

The Activity

Different skills are required in different outdoor activities. A distinction must be made between skills required to safely participate in an activity and those required to master the activity. Mastery is not needed to safely participate if the chosen environment does not demand it. Kayak touring on a small lake requires less skill than kayak touring on the ocean or whitewater kayaking. It is beyond the scope of this book to identify all interactions between environments and activities, so we will assess only the level of skill required to safely perform an activity.

Cognitive ability required for activity. Complex activities that require good memory and integration of many facts may be inappropriate for persons with cognitive impairments. Safe participation in rock climbing, for example, depends on the incorporation of many technical details. A participant may not have to know all these skills, but they must be capable of learning them. The less capable a participant is in assimilating information, the more supervision is required.

Physical ability required for activity. To participate in some activities, individuals must meet basic physical requirements. It is important to know what the critical physical activities are to integrate people with disabilities. Many people may think that to participate on a canoe trip, an individual needs the use of both arms to paddle. In fact, many participate on canoe trips who do not have the use of either arm. Paddling is not a critical factor for participation if the person rides in the middle of a canoe. To be safe and successful, a certain number of people must be able to paddle on the trip (two per canoe), but depending upon the group's size and composition, everyone does not have to paddle.

Cooperation or teamwork. Some activities are solo, whereas others involve teamwork. If participants are to learn an activity that requires teamwork, they must be included with people who have similar or complementary skills or they must be willing to tolerate diversity in physical or cognitive ability.

Time required. Different activities require different lengths of time. A 700-mile Alaskan canoe trip, for example, requires a minimum of 25 days. A five-mile canoe trip on a local river, on the other hand, may be accomplished in an afternoon. Longer activities in remote places require a greater level of knowledge about participants than do short local trips.

The Participants

Attitudes, abilities, and interests of participants are important in successfully integrated programs. The more the service provider knows about the participants, and the participants know about the experience for which they are applying, the greater the chances for success. Participant factors should be considered on both an individual and a group basis. Not only is it important that each person's needs are met, but also that they fit into the group without conflict or undue burden to other group participants.

Functional limitations. The interactions of people with different limitations must be considered when creating the right "mix" of participants. If someone who is blind is paired in a canoe with someone who is deaf, their relative limitations are exacerbated. But a person who is blind may be teamed with a participant using a wheelchair to make their way across a trail. The individual using the wheelchair provides visual support, and the person who is blind can help the other person over rough spots on the trail. In determining how an individual will fit into an integrated outdoor experience, it is helpful to develop guidelines to assess each person's physical ability level as:

— *Physically strong,* adds to physical capacity of group;
— *Physically able,* neither adds nor detracts from physical capacity;
— *Physically semi-dependent,* needs assistance that *may* slow the group; or
— *Physically dependent,* needs assistance that *will* slow the group.

Preparing to snowshoe.

Remember that each person is unique—and may not fit into a single category. But these assessments can help a leader avoid the situation of having an inappropriate number of participants in the physically dependent category.

Degree of self-knowledge. While there is no replacement for staff awareness of participants' health concerns, some come better equipped to take care of themselves than others. A doctor with diabetes is more likely to successfully provide self-care than is an individual who is profoundly mentally retarded. In the case of traumatic injuries, it often takes time for an individual to learn how his/her body responds. Therefore, a man with an acquired disability who has been out of the hospital for ten years is more likely to know his body than one who was discharged just last month. The degree of self-knowledge is important in determining the support necessary for an individual to safely participate in an outdoor education and high adventure activity. People who conduct assessments on an individual's capacity to participate should make an effort to determine how well that individual knows how to meet personal needs.

Levels of special support required by participants. Persons with hearing impairments may require a sign language interpreter, and persons who are unable to attend to personal hygiene needs may require an attendant. Other "regular" participants should never be expected to provide significant levels of special support, because it may detract from their outdoor experience and build resentment toward the person with a disability. In most cases, people who provide this support are either paid or participate in the activity at no (or a reduced) cost.

Abilities of other participants. To be successful, any group in an outdoor education or high adventure activity must *collectively* possess a minimum level of skill to safely enjoy the environment and activities. If seven people take a canoe trip with three canoes, six must be able to paddle. The paddling ability of the seventh person is not especially important from a group safety perspective. A primary consideration in assessing participants, therefore, is the overall level of skill and ability in the group.

Each individual's abilities must be considered in the context of the group. In this sense, integrated groups are often "assembled" with different criteria than segregated groups. Many traditional programs use a "first come, first served" basis. Integrated groups, which must have a minimum number of participants who are capable of safely accomplishing the activities, may use collective group ability as the primary criteria for their assembly.

Motives of participants. As important as participants' abilities are, so too are their motives for participating. Some without disabilities become involved because of misguided altruism to "help the handicapped." Condescension is most frequently found among people who do not have a disability, but it can also be found among those who are disabled but view themselves as "more fortunate" than the next person. Condescension is a barrier to integration because it sets people into different social strata. Assessing teams should be alert to the possibility of condescending attitudes among potential participants and work to alleviate these attitudes by setting non-patronizing examples.

Some may seek to participate because they want to become an expert in the activity or otherwise challenge themselves. These participants can be demanding when it comes to having their needs fulfilled; they pose potential problems for leaders of mixed ability programs where the needs of the many must be balanced with the demands of the few.

Finally, program directors may be surprised to find that not everyone favors social integration, especially if the individual thinks that she or he will lose out somehow in the process. Some people with spinal cord injuries may resent being integrated with persons who are mentally retarded or blind. There are countless reasons why a person with a disability may not want to be integrated with other people who have disabilities, but a few reasons include:

1. Participant needs are viewed as conflicting or incompatible. Persons who use wheelchairs want curb cuts for easier access, but those who are blind do not because they have trouble distinguishing where the sidewalk ends and the street begins.

2. There is a fear that by including a person with a certain disability, another's needs will not be met. No one likes the

idea of having his/her disability exacerbated by the presence of others with different or more severe disabilities.

3. Past negative experiences may inhibit acceptance. One participant of a high adventure trip who used a wheelchair as the result of polio complained about the inclusion of a woman who was mentally retarded. When asked why she objected, she told the trip leaders that during her childhood many people assumed she was "retarded" because she used a wheelchair. She resented that so much that she never wanted to be associated with anyone who had a cognitive disability.

The final example underscores a point about integration. Many people believe that everyone with a disability has an open and accepting attitude toward others with disabilities. Unfortunately, this is not always the case. People with disabilities are, above all else, human. Although not acknowledged by many people in special education, a "pecking order" is sometimes found among persons with disabilities, with people who have cognitive disabilities or disabilities that affect speech at the low end.

Agency Resources

In Chapter 2, the agency's ability to conduct integrated programming in terms of its mission and goals was discussed. Some relevant considerations in assessment are:

Training and skill of staff members. Staff members must fully understand social integration, its value, and the means to achieve it in the specific outdoor activity planned. Thorough staff training allows a greater safety margin in integrated activities because they will be able to compensate for possible screening errors. Another consideration is the physical capabilities of the staff; physically strong leaders have a greater capacity to take persons with mobility impairments to more remote areas.

Until agency staff become familiar with integrated programming, they may consider ranking activities from easy to difficult. Different levels of assessment should be set for each ranking. When applicants for two-hour programs are assessed, issues of personal hygiene are not as important as they are for multi-day adventures. In the same way, assessment for programs that take place in accessible areas may not require as much detail on an individual's capacity to ambulate independently.

Marketing capacity of the agency. Most organizations specialize in a specific clientele. Successfully integrated organizations depend on their ability to attract and hold people from a variety of backgrounds and ability levels. Insufficient enrollment may force the assessment team to accept anyone who comes along, regardless of other factors—which is dangerous and short sighted. Imagine being the only nondisabled person on a kayak trip with people who are quadriplegic. Or, if you are quadriplegic, imagine being the only person with a disability going on the same trip with a group of kayak experts who view you as a nuisance.

Possession of required equipment. By possessing properly adapted equipment, organizations increase their capacity to serve a variety of people. Special seats for canoeing and kayaking, adapted paddles, and pulk sleds are examples of equipment that can facilitate participation by people with disabilities in outdoor adventure programs.

Level of support staff provided by the agency. One issue agency staff will need to address is whether they will accept participants who need a personal care attendant (PCA). Generally, attendants are required when a participant cannot perform bowel or bladder duties, or when they require significant help in personal hygiene. Occasional help dressing, transferring, or with other easy tasks usually does not require an attendant. Another issue is whether an agency will provide sign language interpreters for people with hearing impairments.

Optimal Mix of Participant Abilities
for Integrated High Adventure Programs

Assessing people for integrated adventure programs involves balancing individual and group needs with the demands of the environment. Therefore, each mix of participants depends on the environment and the activity. In general, the best mix of participants includes a person with a disability for every nondisabled person on the trip.

The following mix is used by Wilderness Inquiry for a three- to seven-day canoe trip involving ten people in Minnesota's Boundary Waters Canoe Area Wilderness:

1. Two persons who use wheelchairs. Depending on the physical strength of the leaders and the trip route, people who use wheelchairs generally should weigh less than 165 pounds each. Trips with few or no portages may accommodate wheelchair users who weigh over 200 pounds, especially if they are independent in transferring in and out of their wheelchairs.
2. One or two people with mobility impairments but who are self-ambulatory (*e.g.*, persons whose balance is poor or who use crutches).
3. Two or three people with disabilities that do not affect their ambulation, for example, people who are blind or deaf and people with epilepsy, mild mental retardation, or mild mental illness. For safety reasons, it is recommended that only one person in this category who may experience seizures during the trip be included.
4. Four to five people without disabilities. It is important to try to ascertain their general levels of physical strength and wilderness experiences to determine how much assistance they can provide toward overall group mobility.

Suggested Questions to Ask Applicants of Integrated High Adventure Programs*

In assessing program applicants, begin with an application form that asks a number of questions about an individual's capabilities. The application form should address the assessment factors mentioned earlier in this chapter, especially environment and activity.

---

*These questions were developed by Wilderness Inquiry, Inc., a nonprofit group that provides integrated outdoor adventures throughout the United States for over 2,500 people annually. See Appendix E for an example of their assessment form.

Everyone can contribute in an adventure program.

> *NOTE: Some questions discussed below introduce highly technical health and safety information. This section is intended only as a general introduction to issues frequently addressed in integrated adventure programming. It is NOT intended to provide program staff with a working knowledge of the specific technical issues (e.g., autonomic dysreflexia or decubitus ulcers). Each agency should seek professional medical advice on how these technical issues may affect their programs.*

As indicated earlier, some adventure activities require detailed knowledge of participants while others do not. To ensure safe, quality programming that achieves the goal of social integration, programmers must understand how much information is optimal.

Programmers should also be aware that applicants may answer the same question differently. Most people are honest about themselves, but they may not realize how important details are in forming an integrated group. Others may feel they will be rejected if they tell the truth. Instead of asking only general questions, specific questions also should be asked. Often answers to specific questions alert the person conducting the assessment to issues the applicant has not addressed. If the assessment team suspects that a participant is not giving complete or accurate information, they should check with another reference (*e.g.*, a family member or physician).

Wilderness Inquiry asks the seemingly straightforward question, "Do you have a disability?" An applicant may state that he does not have a disability, but when asked whether he is taking any medication, he will provide a list of medications for seizure control.

Interviews or telephone conversations are important; check with references, including family members or medical professionals. Remember, each person's abilities are unique. In assessing applicants, the goal is to determine the individual's overall ability to safely and successfully participate in the activity. The questions presented below are designed to help assessment teams meet this goal.

Can you walk without assistance? The ability to walk can be interpreted subjectively. Walking in an accessible rehabilitation facility with a cane or walker and in the wilderness are two different skills. If an applicant has a mobility impairment and claims that she can walk, ask questions in the context of the planned activity or environment; can you walk up a steep hill unassisted? On the grass? How is your balance?

Do you use a wheelchair? If an applicant uses a wheelchair, try to determine how strong and coordinated her upper body is. Again, ask questions in the context of the planned activity. How difficult would it be to transfer the applicant in and out of a canoe on a rocky shore with big waves? If applicants are unable to use their wheelchairs effectively on camp sites and trails, would they consider bringing lightweight lawn chairs instead of heavier wheelchairs?

Do you have problems with balance? Poor balance is a common problem. Poor balance may inhibit safe participation depending upon the activity and the environment. Instability in walking due to a disability in the legs may adversely affect hiking or climbing but have no negative impact on canoeing or kayaking. Once the programmer is alerted to the problem, it is often possible to compensate with canes, walkers, and special seating.

Do you have any sensory impairment? Although it may seem redundant, this question is worth asking because many people who are blind or deaf do not consider themselves to have a disability. Persons who need a sign language interpreter to communicate should be provided with one, or they will miss most of the conversation and become socially isolated. Persons who are blind may have a guide dog that they wish to bring on the adventure trip. Lack of skin sensation is common among people with spinal cord injuries, multiple sclerosis, diabetes, and other conditions. Inability to feel can have serious ramifications, especially if the tissue is injured through a burn, abrasion, *etc.*

Do you have problems with pressure sores? Pressure sores (decubitus ulcers) are a serious health concern for people who lack skin sensation. Staff members, including those conducting assessments, should understand the causes, treatments, and effects of pressure sores, or they should probably avoid serving people who have them. A person who frequently experiences pressure sores should be reminded that he will be sleeping on the ground with a sleeping pad, and otherwise be exposed to new situations that will require vigilance to avoid sores. Such a person has to be checked often for situations that may cause sores. *People with existing pressure sores should probably be disqualified from participation in extended adventures due to the risk of infection.*

Have you ever experienced autonomic dysreflexia? This is a potentially life-threatening situation for people with spinal cord injuries. It is triggered by a stimulus to a part of the body below the severed spinal cord—often a blockage in the bladder or bowel, or an injury such as a cut or a burn. *Staff members, including those conducting assessments, should understand the causes, treatments, and effects of autonomic dysreflexia, or they should probably avoid serving people who may experience it.*

What is your exact weight? Some people with disabilities do not know what they weigh. This is an important question for people with mobility impairments because staff members may ultimately be responsible for providing carrying and transferring assistance.

Do you need assistance with eating? Many people, particularly those with cerebral palsy, find eating on adventure trips difficult. Eating from an accessible table is different than eating in the wilderness. If an applicant needs assistance eating at home, they will need it when they are in a wilderness environment.

Do you need assistance with toileting? Toileting is an extremely sensitive issue—staff conducting assessments should use care in discussing this issue. An accessible toilet at the hospital is different from a log in the woods. Collapsible port-a-potties are recommended for people who need significant assistance with toileting.

Many with disabilities have special routines for toileting, especially those who have problems with muscle control. These "bowel programs" often involve the use of enemas or suppositories. An applicant who is not independent in his/her bowel program probably should bring an attendant who is familiar with his/her care.

Another toileting issue is the use of catheters. People who experience a loss of bladder control often use a catheter to urinate. A complete description of the types of catheters is beyond the scope of this book; however, program directors must be certain that they can accommodate the possibility of having a catheter accidentally removed or damaged on a high adventure experience. Applicants should be reminded to bring spare parts and sterile materials they may need.

Have you had any blackouts or seizures in the last two years? Some applicants may have had seizures more than two years ago, but since most states issue a driver's license to an individual who has been seizure-free for two years, this length of time is appropriate for assessment. If the applicant has had blackouts or seizures within the last two years, she should be asked to describe the type, frequency, and possible causes, such as fatigue, flickering sunlight in the trees, or other sensory stimuli. Ask the participant if she has an "aura" or advance warning of an impending seizure. Ask the individual to inform the staff about the warning.

Do you have any dietary restrictions? This question is appropriate for all participants. Sometimes an answer here may indicate a larger problem. An applicant may indicate no disabling conditions on other questions but state that she needs a low-salt diet due to stroke, heart disease, *etc.*

Are you taking any medications? Often people will list medications even though they indicate no specific disability. If medications are listed, find out what purposes they serve. It is also important to determine if an applicant can self-administer them; if not, the participant may need an attendant.

Are you currently under the care of a medical specialist? This question is asked to check the validity of responses to other questions. Some people may not feel that their situation is relevant in other questions but this general question covers a range of issues and prompts participants to think.

Who is completing the form? This question is an important indicator of the reliability of the information. If the form is not completed by the applicant, ask "Why not?"

Other Issues

Although difficult to ask on an application form, those conducting assessments should be alert to signs that may indicate problem behaviors. The social atmosphere of the group is critical to the success of integrated activities. If staff believe that an applicant may have negative behaviors (*e.g.*, violence, severe depression, or sexual inappropriateness), they should investigate further. Those conducting assessments should check with personal references if they believe behavior problems may be an issue.

In integrating outdoor activities, agencies should begin slowly. Easy trips on familiar terrain and assistance from professional medical services, advocacy organizations, and family members will help make initial efforts successful.

Working together to construct a tent shelter.

Chapter Four

PROMOTING SOCIAL INCLUSION AND PERSONAL ACCOMPLISHMENT IN A COOPERATIVE CONTEXT

Society often places too much emphasis on people's limitations rather than their abilities. Charlotte, a nine-year-old with severe mental retardation, was informed by a troop leader that she could not participate in the neighborhood Girl Scout troop. The leader told her family that many motor and cognitive demands were placed on the children to become successful scouts, and Charlotte would be unable to meet these demands. This was unfortunate. Charlotte and her two sisters had spent many days playing by the lake; her sisters had continuously adapted activities to accommodate Charlotte's motor and cognitive abilities.

Similarly, Jon, a 27-year-old with cerebral palsy, had saved money diligently to take a vacation in a national park with an organized singles group. The sponsoring agency was planning a seven-day excursion for young adults to "camp, hike, socialize, and appreciate the outdoors." When Jon's cerebral palsy was discovered by the director on the pre-trip assessment form, he called Jon's group home to inform a care provider that Jon was ineligible and that his money would be refunded. This upset Jon, especially since he had such fond memories of this area from earlier visits. As an adolescent, his peers always managed to identify ways to accommodate him. Unfortunately, as a young adult, his peers appear to be recognizing Jon's limitations and not his strengths. Why?

The tone (philosophy and policies) of outdoor recreation and high adventure programs is set by agency staff. They can mold the norms of a group so that everyone looks for capabilities, not limitations. However, to look at all people positively requires an open mind. And they must believe that the success of every activity depends on everyone making a contribution to the group and to each other's enjoyment. The growing number of integrated outdoor education and high adventure programs throughout the world attest to the fact that many people with disabilities have participatory capabilities.

The suggestions and techniques discussed in this chapter involve three topics related to emphasizing abilities:

1. Establishing ground rules for how people should value each person's contribution to a group.

2. Building individuals into a team.

3. Using strategies to promote team and individual benefits.

Establishing Ground Rules for How People Should Value Each Person's Contribution to a Group

Although outdoor education, high adventure, and recreation agencies must assume leadership in assuring equal access to services, "key" individuals, such as group home staff members, parents, care providers, and teachers, must participate in the integration process. When bringing together agencies, professionals, and families to promote integrated programs, the program director and staff play a crucial role and should model the following values:

Show personal humility. A humble approach gains more respect and cooperation from participants and co-workers than a haughty one. The most respected experts in any field are those who are not afraid to ask questions and are the first to criticize their own work.

Do not make a priori assumptions about participants' abilities. Directors should not view participants as sick, maladjusted, or in need of some magic outdoor education or high adventure counseling. They must not assume that people are incapable of taking decisive action or making informed decisions. While some participants may be emotionally unbalanced or intellectually disabled, most of these conditions will be known from the application form (see Chapter 3). Other participants may have problems (poor judgment is not confined to people with disabilities) that become apparent only after observation in the outdoor environment. People with disabilities should be viewed as more "typical" than "special." And, directors should never make the mistake of thinking that everyone needs emotional or psychological help—they do not.

Have a strong interest in group process. A democratic process is recommended as long as safety and essential logistics are not compromised. Participants should be treated as mature people who can make rational decisions; all should be involved in making daily decisions about where to go, what to do, and what to eat. Their opinions *do* matter.

Emphasize the value of attitude, expenditure of effort, and nonphysical accomplishments. In an outdoor setting, many people have a tendency to measure their "value" according to their ability to perform physical tasks. One of the greatest challenges faced by staff during mixed-ability outdoor adventures is to counter that all-too-common idea. Meeting this challenge is complicated because such settings are generally less accessible for people with disabilities. People with mobility or sensory impairments are often less able to make tangible physical contributions on the trail than they are at home. To prevent reinforcing perceived limitations, the director and staff must take the attitude that the adventure is a learning experience for everyone.

Many people with disabilities have been told throughout their lifetimes that they cannot do certain things. In some cases, the statement may be justified. But too much emphasis has been placed on limitations, rather than strengths and possibilities. The world is full of stories of people who were told they could not do something but went out and did it anyway. After discussing the Edisons, Einsteins, FDRs, and Beethovens of the world, staff members can initiate an exercise in which participants are asked to share what they consider to be their greatest achievements.

Everyone has limitations. However, most people, not just those with disabilities, underutilize their personal resources and are afraid to test their limits. Once participants start thinking differently about physical accomplishments and challenges, they are less likely to measure their worth to the group along traditional, physically-oriented benchmarks.

In a real sense, an able-bodied person who carries a pack but only exerts a fraction of her/his ability is worth "less" to the group than an individual with a mobility impairment who crawls across the trail while operating at 110 percent. Failing is not important—trying is. It is far more important for participants to use their effective skills than to lament about what they do not have. This point is essential in establishing the basis for integrating people of varying ability levels.

It is also critical to stress attitude. A funny joke or a smile under adverse physical conditions does more to boost group morale than sheer muscle power. Sweet or sour, individual attitudes are contagious in a group. An individual's attitude is probably the most important group contribution. This is not to suggest that physical accomplishments are unimportant—without them, the group will not go far. But physical accomplishments must take their place alongside a positive attitude and expenditure of effort.

Respect each person's dignity. This seemingly obvious suggestion is a key to successful social integration. Once group members understand that they are accepted and respected for who they are, they will participate more readily in attaining group goals. In mixed-ability groups, the process of developing mutual respect is complicated by unfamiliarity with different participant needs and expectations. It is easy to make wrong assumptions about what a person actually needs in a given situation.

Respecting dignity begins with avoiding any personal gesture that suggests a condescending attitude. Too many well-meaning but unthinking people develop a patronizing or condescending attitude toward those whom they consider to be "less fortunate." Condescension may also exist among people with different disabilities. Those who have cognitive or developmental disabilities sometimes have trouble being accepted by people who have physical disabilities only. Persons who experience speech and communication difficulties also may experience acceptance problems that transcend their disability.

All these behaviors could be considered efforts by those who discriminate to elevate their own status by disassociating themselves from people whom they consider to be less capable. Although it seems contradictory, condescending behavior is motivated on the one hand by the desire to help, and on the other, by the desire to elevate one's own perceived status. Condescending attitudes may be extremely subtle and difficult to identify. And once identified, they are awkward to point out. The well-intentioned "offender" may be hurt if her/his efforts to "help" are misunderstood. People who manifest a condescending attitude are unlikely to accept the argument that they were really trying to elevate their own status. Thus, rather than confronting the offender directly, sometimes it is better to let a situation pass and to return to the issue at a more appropriate moment.

A helpful guide to identifying condescending attitudes is to think of the differences in behavior appropriate for interaction with a young child and with an adult. The following examples illustrate this point:

— *Tokenism.* Sometimes in their desire to get people involved, inexperienced staff members complete a task and then give credit to a person with a disability who simply observed. A group collects firewood, cuts it, sets the fire up, and then gives a match to a person with a disability to light the fire. After the twigs are set ablaze, staff members compliment the person for having "made" such a wonderful fire.

— *Tangible contribution.* Another staff member with the same goal searched for methods to promote appropriate involvement. A woman with cerebral palsy who uses a wheelchair was able to hold the log and stabilize it while it was being sawed. After it was cut, she put on a pair of gloves and broke off twigs and small branches, putting them aside for kindling. It took her longer, but she made a genuine contribution. After the fire was lit, she was thanked for her help in a tone of voice that indicated the same level of appreciation offered to any adult. There was no exaggerated sense of surprise and no obsequious praise.

The basis for respect is the recognition that everyone needs purpose and meaning in their lives. What really counts is not what you have, but how you use it. Often, in the rush to get things done expediently, there is a temptation to adopt the quickest and physically easiest solution. But in arranging adaptations, the director and staff should consider safe options to avoid compromising a participant's dignity. Some situations may demand unglamorous solutions, but they are relatively few. Addressing potentially unglamorous adaptations openly and in advance with the person involved may stimulate suggestions and gain acceptance for a solution. Ideally, this process should begin before the individual even registers for the trip.

Building Individuals into a Team

Authentic espirit de corps does not occur by chance. It is forged out of desire (sometimes out of need), reaching its zenith when individuals take their pleasure from seeing the group succeed rather than focusing on their own success. Integrated groups contain the team spirit spark, and individual diversity has a natural inclination to ignite. But often group strategies are needed to fan the spark and channel its energy. Three team-building processes are recommended as follows.

A classroom in the outdoors.

Topical Discussion Groups

Communication is essential to integrating people with diverse backgrounds and abilities into a group. Some people may experience frustration if they are not fully independent during certain activities, especially those with mobility impairments. Inform each group, at the outset, that personal independence/mobility is an issue that can be discussed openly. Encourage each participant to suggest ways in which they can participate more fully.

Encourage honest discussions about needs and expectations. Disclosing personal information may represent an emotional risk for persons with disabilities. Staff members can help by disclosing a few of their own needs, making it clear that everyone is accepted, regardless of her/his situation. From the applications and pre-screening, staff members should already understand specific physical and emotional/social needs of every participant. If these needs are not shared voluntarily during introductory group discussions, staff members must choose to push for disclosure or to let it pass for future discussion. This decision, of course, depends on the situation. For example, night blindness or a bladder infection does not necessarily need to be shared with the group. However, if an evening activity is planned or others cannot understand why someone is drinking large quantities of water and making frequent toilet stops, then disclosing such facts may be advisable.

On issues such as time-consuming personal hygiene needs, personal feelings may become more emotionally charged. Staff members must approach these situations with sensitivity and in a straightforward manner. "Jon, do you have any personal routines that we should know about in planning our schedule for tomorrow? Can we break camp at 7 a.m., or do you need more time?" When questions are asked in a straightforward manner and for a good reason, most people will respond openly and honestly.

In a rush to make dozens of small decisions in quick succession, staff members are susceptible to acting autonomously instead of seeking input from all participants. Although faster, autonomous decisions do not inspire individuals to accept the decisions. Staff members should discuss how decisions will be made at the start of the trip. The choices range from autocratic, to consensus, to simple majority. Choosing the appropriate style depends on the situation. If safety is an issue (*e.g.*, paddling in a strong wind), an autocratic style may work best. The opinion of the group can and should be sought beforehand, but ultimately, safety decisions must be made by the staff. On the other hand, in deciding which route to take, group consensus may be best because participants are then more likely to "buy into" the decision. If a decision is simply whether to have lentil soup tonight or tomorrow night, a majority probably will suffice. Staff members influence the outcome of any decision by choosing the parameters. By actively soliciting opinions of all participants before making final decisions, staff members can facilitate social integration. In effect, when participants perceive that they have an equal say in decisions, the concept of equal peer status is enhanced.

The McGill Action Planning System

The McGill Action Planning System (MAPS) is useful for creating a long-term plan for an individual with a disability. It is a transition strategy that assists parents, outdoor educators, the child with a disability, peers, *etc.*, to plan collaboratively for the future. MAPS planning often occurs in one or two sessions. Participants usually are arranged in a half-circle, with the facilitator positioned at the open end. Information and ideas generated from the process are recorded on large chart paper. The chart serves as a communication check during the session and as a record when the planning is completed. The role of the facilitator is to solicit participation of all team members in designing a community-use plan for the student, one that features integration (Vandercook & York, 1989).

Seven questions comprise the MAPS process:

1. *What is the individual's history?* Family members (and the individual with a disability, as much as possible) are asked to talk about the individual's life history and expectations for future developmental milestones.

2. *What is your dream?* This question forces team members to identify the direction in which they are heading with the individual; only then can specific plans be made. Of course, visions, plans, or expectations are not set in concrete; they are challenged continually as more is learned about how to facilitate the individual's inclusion in the community. It may be difficult to envision adult dreams for a young child; if that is a problem, team members can be encouraged to think just a few years ahead.

3. *What is your nightmare?* This is a difficult question to ask, especially for parents, yet it is extremely important. Once a nightmare is exposed, team members must work hard to keep it from happening. Interestingly, parents frequently see the nightmare as a vision of their child being alone.

4. *Who is the individual?* Participants are asked to think of words that describe the individual. There are no "right" or "wrong" words. Each participant around the circle speaks in turn until all thoughts have been expressed. When the list is complete, the facilitator asks certain people, usually family members and peers, to identify approximately three words from the list that they feel describe the individual best.

5. *What are the individual's strengths, gifts, and abilities?* The facilitator asks participants to review the word list and to identify some strengths and unique gifts. In addition, they are instructed to think about what the individual especially likes to do and does particularly well.

6. *What are the individual's needs?* This question provides an opportunity for team members to identify needs from various perspectives. When the list is complete, team members are asked to order needs by their importance. The lists of assets and identified needs become an important basis for designing the outdoor education program.

7. *What would the individual's ideal day (at the nature center, etc.) look like, and what must be done to make it happen?* Because MAPS is oriented toward planning for integrating individuals with disabilities into regular, age-appropriate settings,

attention to this question begins by outlining a day in that setting for a nondisabled peer. Next, the team begins to develop ways that the identified needs can be met in the context of the programmed day. Finally, the supports needed to achieve successful integration are outlined.

The MAPS process provides a "road map" for team members to be supportive and effective in integrating participants with disabilities into school and community life. Susan exemplifies the process.

Susan has Rett syndrome and requires assistance to participate in and contribute to a neighborhood 4-H club. When the time came for her to join a club, it was very important to her parents that she attend one with nondisabled children. The chosen club emphasized such outdoor activities as nature study and camping.

Susan has many friends in her neighborhood. But Debbie, Nancy, and Patricia, nondisabled 4-H club members, are her closest friends. Toward the end of last year, Susan's 4-H leader decided to design club meetings that gave her more opportunities to participate. MAPS was used to assist in this goal. The planning team included family members, the 4-H leader, special educators, therapists, peers, and Susan. The MAPS process helped deepen relationships between Susan and her friends. Debbie, Nancy, and Patricia got to know her family, her developmental history, and her needs from other perspectives. Her friends were recognized as valued, contributing members of Susan's team.

One of the first questions asked in the MAPS process was, "What is your dream for Susan as an adult?" Susan's mother hoped that Susan as an adult would live with friends that she cared about and who cared about her. Debbie said that she hoped that she, Nancy, and Patricia could be Susan's friends always. The dream question in the MAPS process was followed by the difficult question, "What is your nightmare?" Susan's mother responded that Susan would be very lonely as an adult. The responses to these two questions illustrate why friendship is important—it is a step toward the dream and away from the nightmare.

One of the last questions asked during the MAPS process was, "What are Susan's needs?" One need identified by the 4-H leader was that other people accept and deal with Susan's drooling (she drools a lot). Her friends, matter of factly and comfortably, addressed the need saying that they would remove her bandana periodically to help her wipe her mouth or chin.

The descriptor most frequently used now in describing Susan's inclusion in regular 4-H activities with her peers is "happy." In fact, the first phrase that comes to mind for everyone, including the county 4-H director is, "Susan and her friends are so happy now!"

Circle of Friends

Circle of Friends is a team-building process that is often used with individuals who have widely differing abilities and have not worked and played together as a team. According to O'Brien, Forest, Snow, and Hasbury (1989), it represents a support group—a circle of friends who create a place of listening and welcome, a place where people grow in affection toward and respect for the individual with a disability (and each other), and a place where nondisabled friends challenge friends with disabilities to increase their skills.

Circle of Friends needs an adult facilitator to launch it (and later, to keep it from sinking). Before a new student with a disability joins an integrated group, the facilitator invites several nondisabled children to become the core of the new individual's circle of friends. The facilitator begins by telling them a story about the new person, often using information from the MAPS session. Nondisabled participants then discuss ways they can build the new individual's strengths, solve problems presented by integration, *etc.* (Perske & Perske, 1988; Schleien, Fahnestock, Green, & Rynders, 1990).

The children then meet as a circle of friends and the "story" continues to unfold, always featuring the dream for the individual. Eventually, a plan for integration is constructed and the individuals' parts are determined under the guidance of the facilitator. The plan often includes the following steps (oriented for our purposes toward an outdoor education class conducted in a nearby nature center):

1. *Plan a welcome* about a week before the student with a disability will join the class. (The student with a disability does not participate in this meeting.) If inclusion is new to the nature center, the director's participation in the meeting sends a message about its importance.

2. *Orient the class to integration.* Contrast integration and segregation; show the disadvantages of segregation and identify benefits of integration. Show how segregated settings reinforce stereotypes. Discuss negative consequences of stereotyping.

3. *Clarify the ground rules for inclusion.* Acknowledge adult fears. "We—the parents of the new student, the teachers, the director, the integration facilitator—are scared about the student with special needs joining your nature study class. Why do you think we are scared?" Discussing this question gives class members an opportunity to clarify boundaries of acceptable behavior toward the individual with special needs and defines students as a resource to the adults. Take time to discuss the following questions with the class, keeping written notes about participants' ideas. What are some things that would hurt the class's welcome to the new person? What can you do to include the new person, making the new person feel welcome? What should the first day be like? Clarify the nondisabled participants' roles as classmates and potential friends, not parents or teachers.

4. *Highlight the importance of good relationships and friendships in everyone's life.* Ask students to identify important relationships in their lives by putting people's names in each of four concentric circles (Figure 4.1). Pass out a circle to each person, saying:

   — "In the center circle, put the names of the people closest to you—the people you love and count on the most."

   — "In the second circle, put names of people you really like and count on, but not quite as much as those you put in the first circle."

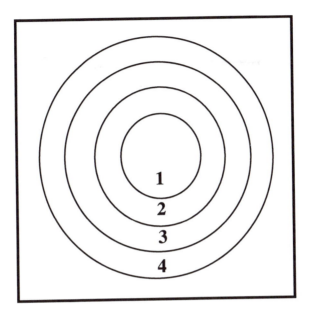

Figure 4.1. Concentric circles identify relationships.

— "In the third circle, put the names of groups of people you know and like to do things with, like scouts, swimming, sports, clubs, and so on."

— "In the fourth circle, put the names of people who get paid to be in your life, like your doctor, dentist, therapeutic recreation specialist, and others like that."

Ask for volunteers to name some people they put in each circle and ask what they do with them. Show a contrasting set of circles for someone with few relationships. "Joe is your age. He has only his mom in circle one and the rest of his circles are empty, except for circle four. His circle four is filled with doctors, therapists, and social workers. How would you feel if your life looked like this?" Underscore the importance of people with whom to do things. Affirm the participants' capacity to give friendship to another and to the participant with a disability. Recognize that friendship grows with time and usually begins with shared activities. Not everyone will be close friends with the new nature class member but everyone can be friendly.

5. *Organize a welcoming committee.* Committee members agree to help the new participant feel welcome in the class by greeting; orienting her/him to where things are, the routine, and activities; inviting her/him to take part in classroom, lunch time, and break activities; helping with safety around the pond; *etc.*

6. *Set up a telephone committee.* Identify class members who will phone the student with a disability to talk about what happened today and what will happen tomorrow. Find a participant for each night of the week.

7. *Participants may have questions about the special needs of their new classmate,* particularly if responding to needs that change their daily routine. Keep information practical and factual; this is not the occasion for a mini-lecture on the neurology of cerebral palsy or the genetics of Down syndrome. Encourage participants to pursue questions with resource people, such as the new person, parents, or nature study personnel.

8. *Let participants know about the availability of resource people.* Tell the class when, for example, a therapeutic recreation specialist or physical therapist is coming to teach class members how to help their classmate with special needs.

To illustrate, Joe, a child with a moderate degree of mental retardation and physical limitations, was supported by the Circle of Friends. During the first meeting, the circle understood that Joe and his parents wanted an integrated experience on a weekly basis at the nature center. The circle began their planning under the facilitative nurturing of Dorothy, the nature center director. After meeting twice—once with Joe's parents who talked about their dream and once with the facilitator and the parents for the problem-solving exercise—they discussed activities at the nature center that would be age-appropriate for Joe and within his capabilities and physical limitations (Joe has lower limb mobility problems; he walks with a special cane).

Joe's new circle of friends, doing some creative thinking, concluded that an activity they could all enjoy together was cultivating, planting, and selling herbs. Mindful of Joe's limitations, the group figured out how to elevate the plant beds so he could sift soil, plant seeds, *etc.*, without bending over. Dorothy structured the group for cooperative outcomes (see Using Cooperative Grouping Arrangements Successfully in this chapter). Everyone in the group would have to contribute to planting, *etc.*, to share in the profits from the herb sale; the group selected someone to verify in writing everyone's involvement.

After many weeks of planting, weeding, watering, and fertilizing, group participants picked the herbs and sold them in collaboration with a local shopping mall, taking turns selling the plants and helping Joe when it was his turn to be at the sales table. The group did not make much money, but earned enough for pizzas (with special herbs on them of course) in a celebration party at the nature center. The Circle of Friends program has been so successful that the nature center receives numerous requests (mostly from nondisabled individuals) to join the program next year. Hence, Dorothy has decided to operate two circles of friends next year.

Supporting Curriculum to Enhance Friendship

Use of the *Special Friends* curriculum (Voeltz *et al.*, 1983) or companionship training programs (Rynders & Schleien, 1991) can enhance the knowledge and motivation of participants without disabilities. These materials are often used for short (15-30 minutes) informal group discussions between interaction sessions. Suggested topics from the curriculum include:

— *How do we participate together?* Discuss how friends take turns, say nice things to each other, help each other when a task is difficult, stay close to each other when playing, smile at each other, and so forth. Reinforce interaction techniques.

— *How do we communicate?* Discuss communication tips, such as talking slowly, allowing time for a response, trying another way if your friend does not understand you, and not giving up. Common, simple manual signs (*e.g.*, hello, good, want, you, and me) can be introduced.

— *What is a prosthesis?* Discuss the use of tools (*e.g.*, fishing pole or net) that people without disabilities need to perform certain tasks (*e.g.*, catch a fish). Show examples of a prosthesis (*e.g.*, an artificial limb) and explain how it is like a tool for people who have lost a limb.

— *How does a person with a disability live in the community?* Invite a person who is disabled to come and discuss how she travels from home to work, goes camping, snowshoeing, *etc.*

— *What is a best friend?* Discuss friendship. Ask participants to think about similarities and differences in their relationship with their friend with a disability and their best friend (if not the same person).

There are several ways to use companionship training curricula in the outdoor environment. Their use depends on the type of center or environment, the characteristics of participants, and time available. If the program provides the outdoor educator or naturalist more time with the integrated group, through a progressive course or residential program, an extensive (i.e., ongoing) companionship training curriculum can be beneficial.

Selected activities make participants aware of some difficulties that peers with disabilities experience. Blindfolding nondisabled participants for a guided hike in the woods can help them to understand the limitations and obstacles experienced by someone who is visually impaired. Tying nondisabled participants' hands behind their backs and asking them to carry items to a particular location can help them understand carrying problems. Describe prostheses animals use—how monkeys poke twigs into ants' nests and how gulls drop shellfish from heights to get at the meat. These activities and discussions help to explain that both animals and people possess different skills, abilities, and forms of adaptation. These training exercises could lead to a greater understanding and empathy, and result in a positive experience for all participants.

The following goals, activity ideas, and questions have been developed for outdoor educators or naturalists when preparing persons without disabilities for an integrated program.

Goals:

1. To understand characteristics of friendship.

2. To compare and contrast friendships of persons with and without disabilities.

3. To become familiar with materials and activities that will be used during companionship interactions.

4. To learn about alternatives and adaptations when participating in activities with peers who have disabilities.

Activities:

1. Ask participants to define a friend by completing the statement, "A friend is . . . "

2. Discuss different types of friendship:

    — Best friends.

    — Children of their parents' friends who come to visit occasionally.

    — Individuals in the neighborhood they may spend time with after school or after work.

    — Students or employees they see often at school or work.

3. Ask individuals to think about their best friends and the things they do together; then think about the things they do with their companion(s) with disabilities.

4. Discuss similarities and differences between friendships with their best friends and with their companions.

   — What nice feelings do they have from interacting with both types of friends?

   — Are their feelings for companions different from their feelings for other friends? If so, why?

5. Interact with an individual with a disability, or have a teacher, parent, or sibling, who knows that individual well, demonstrate ways to:

   — Gain the attention of an individual who is developmentally disabled.

   — Physically guide her/him to or through an activity.

   — Take turns with that person.

   — Share with that person.

   — Let that person know you like her and that she is interacting appropriately.

6. Demonstrate communication devices and methods, such as cues.

7. Show individuals some materials that will be used in activities and ask how they would work cooperatively with their companions to complete the activities.

Specific examples:

1. Ask participants how a person in a wheelchair can help find hidden animals in the forest.

2. Ask participants to think of ideas to modify a fishing rod so that a person with motor difficulties can grasp the rod.

3. Ask participants how they would hide in the forest with someone who is in a wheelchair.

4. Ask participants how they might help a person who has a hearing impairment and is mentally retarded locate and experience things.

5. Ask participants how they would help a friend who is visually impaired identify animals from fur samples.

Using Strategies to Promote Team and Individual Benefits

With a positive attitude for integration and dynamic group processing strategies, the program director and staff are ready to implement specific cooperative strategies. These programmatic strategies will help participants identify their roles and responsibilities during the integrated experiences. Also, these "best professional practices" should promote cooperative participation and the making of friends.

Develop Symbiotic Relationships Among Participants

Symbiotic implies that participants function together in a *mutually beneficial* relationship but also develop their skills as individuals (Green, 1982). In each group, there is the potential to team people with differing abilities together to get a job done.

1. A person with visual or balance problems can be teamed with one who uses a wheelchair to cross portages. The walker can push the wheelchair when needed, while the wheelchair provides stability. The person in the wheelchair can serve as the "eyes" for a person who is blind. *Be sure to assess the safety of the trail first.*

2. A person who is unable to carry a pack may be able to help steady someone with poor balance or serve as the "eyes" for someone who is blind. This mutuality works on portages, in camp, *etc.*

3. A person who experiences seizures or who is mentally re-
    tarded may be able to help guide someone who is blind.

4. An older or younger participant can help stabilize someone
    who has trouble walking.

5. A person who uses a wheelchair can help someone who is
    hemiplegic and needs help dressing.

6. A person who is unable to carry heavy loads may help
    someone else eat or get dressed. Ask them to do so, if
    necessary, but always check with the proposed recipient of
    the assistance as well.

There are many other situations where the team approach—
each person using her/his specific abilities—allows the accomplishment of difficult goals. The approach is especially effective
if the staff can team two people together who require different
kinds of assistance to accomplish a given task. In promoting and
arranging symbiotic relationships, staff members must recognize that every participant must make a contribution to the
group's welfare to achieve equal status in the team.

---

*While on a Boundary Waters Canoe Area Wilderness canoe trip, an
ambitious group decided to "bushwack" an unmarked portage trail from
one lake to the next at night. The distance was over a mile, up and down
hills, over bogs, and through thick brush. It was decided to conduct the
portage in stages: advancing to a point, leaving the gear, and returning
for another load. It soon became clear that there was a real possibility of
being unable to find the advance pile of equipment on the second trip.
The group attempted to figure out how to solve the problem. One person
with a mobility impairment suggested that he and the others who were
mobility impaired be stationed along the trail to provide an "audio
beacon" for those carrying the gear. One person who had polio was left
with the initial pile of equipment, and another person with multiple
sclerosis made her way to the advance station where the gear would be
placed. By singing, telling jokes, and generally raising a ruckus, they
were able to effectively guide those who were carrying packs and canoes.*

This example demonstrates a creative team approach to solving a problem by using the capabilities that each participant possesses. Staff members should keep in mind that arranging mutually beneficial task relationships is a skill that requires a constant search for the right fit of abilities and tasks.

Delegate Tasks

It is easier to talk about processes in the abstract than it is to act on the ideas, but specific and concrete action is often needed. Staff members must know how to break down any group task into attainable steps, and at least initially be prepared to delegate these steps to appropriate participants.

Tokenism must be avoided. The responsibility a staff member delegates must be a legitimate function or the individuals involved will see through it easily. Staff members can delegate functions judicially. A person with a disability can be asked to lead a problem-solving discussion, plot the route, and decide what to eat and how to cook it. By assigning important and functional tasks, people will respond. Staff members should be careful, however, not to set up participants for failure or for challenges from other participants.

Many programs rotate tasks among group members; each participant is expected to take part in a given activity, such as washing dishes or putting equipment away, an equal number of times. This system works well when all members are capable of performing the same tasks. However, when people are unable, physically or cognitively, to perform similar tasks, a rotation system can skew the workload toward the more physically or intellectually capable and discourage contributions from less-able participants.

In a mixed-ability group, it may be necessary for certain people to perform the same tasks throughout the program. Someone who can participate only in limited areas should be allowed freedom of choice to participate as often as the task must be performed. For some participants, this may mean cutting wood, carrots, or bread; for others, it may be helping with dishes. If a staff member suspects that someone is suffering from the "excess baggage syndrome" (feeling left out), she or he should

ask the participant to help with a task the participant can perform.

In delegating tasks, staff members must identify the components of specific activities and break them into units that allow
participation by people with varying abilities. The following
illustration shows an analysis for a canoeing activity.

1. Basic travel.

    a. Paddling canoes.
    b. Loading and unloading canoes.
    c. Portaging and carrying.
    d. Navigation.

2. Camp chores and activities.

    a. Building and maintaining fires and/or stoves (see
        detailed description on next page).
    b. Food preparation and clean-up.
    c. Setting up tents.
    d. Latrines.
    e. Camp clean up and restoration.
    f. Procuring water for group.
    g. Sawing wood.
    h. Providing feeding assistance.
    i. Moderating discussions.

3. Personal needs.

    a. Feeding assistance.
    b. Medications.
    c. Washing clothes and hair.
    d. Mobility.
    e. Assistance dressing.
    f. Hygiene and toileting.

4. Safety.

    a. Observing safety policies.
    b. Keeping canoes in close formation while traveling.

    c. Extinguishing fires.
    d. Weather observation.

5. Other activities.

    a. Wildlife identification.
    b. Plant identification.
    c. Moderating discussions.
    d. Fishing.
    e. Minimum impact practices.
    f. Repairing clothes and equipment.

Each component can, in turn, be broken down into smaller tasks. To illustrate, we analyze the process of fire building and maintenance and relate specific components to potential individual assignments.

Components of building and maintaining fires:

    a. Selecting fire site.
    b. Obtaining firewood.
    c. Sawing firewood.
    d. Trimming twigs from sawed logs.
    e. Collecting kindling—twigs, birch bark, leaves, or grass.
    f. Arranging materials for optimal combustion.
    g. Applying match or lighter.
    h. Fanning flames or coals (if necessary).
    i. Adding fuel (wood) as needed.
    j. Protecting wood from rain.
    k. Extinguishing fire.
    l. Possibly dismantling fire site.

It is possible to integrate persons with various abilities in some or all components of this activity by forming symbiotic teams. People who have control of their upper bodies can usually saw logs, trim twigs, collect and prepare kindling, arrange materials, keep the fire burning, add fuel, and extinguish, and possibly, dismantle the fire ring. Someone with a visual impairment usually can help with all the tasks depending on the degree of impairment. Persons who have uncontrolled movement or spasticity in their limbs may not be able to safely operate a saw, but they can strip twigs or secure the log for someone else to saw. Participants with intellectual disabilities can participate actively in all or most aspects of the program, with appropriate training and/or support.

Most tasks can be broken down into components that "fit" a person's abilities or strengths. Two or three people can team up to successfully complete a job. With each tangible contribution to the process, the goal of integration is more fully achieved.

Components of canoe portaging serve as an example of this process for major tasks. Portaging in a wilderness canoe area is a challenge for everyone. It requires movement of people and equipment across a trail between two bodies of water. The trails can be long or short, flat or steep, and are often full of rocks or boggy areas. Depending on the route, portaging easily presents the greatest physical challenge on any canoe trip. Hence, it is helpful to get participants prepared emotionally for the challenge. Let them know that it will be hard work for everyone, and that successful completion of the portage will require each person to give what he can toward the crossing. Some discomfort is part of the process and everyone is likely to feel it. But the individual and group rewards are worthwhile.

Portaging techniques that work well with mixed-ability groups include:

1. Persons who walk slowly or who need significant assistance in walking should start down the trail first. This allows them more time to complete the trail while others carry equipment across. If a person can cross a trail independently, allow her or him the time to do so.

2. Encourage participants in wheelchairs to go as far as they can safely on their own. Then, as persons carrying packs and canoes walk back and forth, they can help the wheelchair users over difficult spots.

3. Participants should set off in groups, with people matched according to their abilities. Persons who are unable to carry heavy physical loads can act as visual assistants and support

people, or they can carry smaller items such as day packs or paddles.

4. Some persons who are blind or who lack balance can team up with a wheelchair user to push their way across (see Develop Symbiotic Relationships Among Participants in this chapter). If a trail is too rough to allow persons with mobility impairments to cross independently, they may have to be carried (see Chapter 5). Being carried across a trail may contribute to the "excess baggage syndrome." Persons who must be carried can be given tasks, such as passing out water or treats at the end of the trail, organizing gear on the other side, or stationing themselves at forks in the trail to show the correct route.

Other examples of task delegation occurred on a demanding trip. During a high adventure trip, a person fell on a tent and ripped it. A staff member asked who in the group could sew. An elderly woman in a wheelchair volunteered eagerly. She was given the sewing kit and then proceeded to fix every tear—in every tent, life-jacket, and pack.

A woman with cerebral palsy was able to carry packs, but her hands were too spastic to allow her to eat with utensils. She helped push another person in a wheelchair who, in turn, helped her to eat her soup each evening.

Some people are quite skilled at moderating discussions and conducting group sensitization exercises. This skill does not require mobility. If a participant does have these skills, staff members may encourage their use in an appropriate setting.

A participant with multiple sclerosis was upset throughout the trip because he became aware of how much function and control he had lost. Staff members tried to comfort him, but they could not empathize completely with his condition. A woman who was quadriplegic and unable to help with physical tasks volunteered to comfort him. She was sincere and skilled, and the effect was successful. No staff member or other participant could have done a better job at helping the man to accept his condition and to make the most of it.

* * *

A man who was severely affected by cerebral palsy and used a communication board shared his philosophy of life with the group. He had a dramatic effect on several participants and the staff. This man used to walk and talk but he had occasional spasms. As a ward of the state, he consented to an operation that would rehabilitate him. A medical team drilled two holes in his head and performed a lobotomy, accidentally taking away his speech and his ability to walk; the spasms remained. His acceptance and his will to live were truly inspirational and made everyone forget about their aching bodies.

* * *

A participant who had had a stroke revealed that he had served in Vietnam. In the middle of a difficult portage, one person asked him if he had killed anyone. Understandably, the man was upset by the question. It was a tense, awkward moment. A woman who was blind, a speech pathologist, took the man by the hand and asked him to forgive the thoughtless comment and the awful injustice of the war. They walked for a short distance and talked. That night the man told a heart-rending saga of his experiences, and the group came away with a new understanding of war, the plight of veterans with disabilities, and of the man himself.

These examples of allowing and encouraging participants to team up and use their skills and abilities demonstrate that an individual's "worth" to a group is not limited to what she/he can carry. In each case, significant contributions to the group welfare were made by persons who did not fit the rugged "wilderness traveler" image.

Determine Desired Roles of Participants

The outdoor activity leader should not only be clear about the primary purpose of activities, but also the desired roles of nondisabled participants in interactions with peers who have disabilities. The leader must determine whether the nondisabled participants will be interacting as *friends, tutors,* or *both.* Each role fits a slightly different goal. However, all roles fit into a *cooperative* learning orientation.

In a *peer-tutor* program, a peer without a disability teaches a skill to one with a disability. The relationship of peers in a tutoring program can be thought of as "vertical," that is, the tutor is in charge ("I'm the teacher, you're the pupil"). For example, a 12-year-old child without disabilities comes to a nature center and works one-to-one teaching fishing skills to a 6-year-old child with a disability. The older child gives systematic training and practice to the younger one. The child with a disability should not always be involved in outdoor educational or recreational activities as the one who receives "help," which is often a prevalent expectation in tutoring programs. It is important for a child with a disability to experience giving as well as receiving.

A *peer-friend* program promotes positive social interactions (friendliness) between a person with a disability and one without. Peers should be approximately the same age, although the individual without a disability can be one or two years older than the person with a disability. (It can be socially awkward if the person with a disability is older than the peer friend.) This relationship is "horizontal," that is, a relatively equal, turn-taking relationship ("I'm your friend, you're my friend"). A typical application is one in which two peers, one with a disability and one without, make a campfire by taking turns preparing wood for the fire, lighting the campfire with two matches, and enjoying it together.

At first, it may appear that the choice between these two peer roles (tutor and friend) is easy and tailored according to the outcome desired—skill acquisition or socialization. A peer-tutor is used if the primary objective is acquisition of specific skills; a peer-friend is used if socialization is the main objective. But making a choice between the two is not generally necessary. Instead, activity leaders can facilitate friendship initially. Later, it is normal for one friend to teach another to play a new outdoor game or for both to participate in an outdoor education activity, thus allowing skill acquisition to occur in the natural course of the friendship (Rynders & Schleien, 1991).

Recruit Nondisabled Peers and Strengthen Friendship Skills

A helpful tool to recruit nondisabled participants is a slide presentation* illustrating interactions of people with and without disabilities in integrated outdoor education activities and on high adventure trips. Such a presentation provides a positive image for prospective participants, many of whom may have negative images of integrated outdoor programs due to their limited exposure to persons who have disabilities. Recruitment presentations that depict positive interactions help create the expectation that they also will have a positive experience. That expectation alone can go a long way toward creating a successful program.

Why should an activity leader spend time giving instruction in friendship? Don't people without disabilities naturally interact in a friendly way with those who have disabilities? Yes and no. Yes, they usually know how to be friendly (although they may need to have friendship skills sharpened or expanded). And no, peers without disabilities do not often have the knowledge and skills to interact easily with a person who has a disability. A disabling condition presents interaction challenges never experienced directly by peers without disabilities. Participants without disabilities may need instruction in how to cope with communication, social, movement, and other types of challenges.

Meetings involving nondisabled group members and leaders can occur immediately before and/or after an integrated session. Focus discussion on how to overcome a particular interaction problem, new ideas for interacting, and specific techniques for one-to-one activities. Engage participants in problem solving based on ideas for activity modification. They can think out loud about how to modify a pond study so that a person with cerebral palsy can participate despite limited arm and hand use. When peers without disabilities apply themselves to enhance the participation of a partner with a disability, it builds empathy, self-awareness, and maturity.

Photo Use Permit. If you make your own slides, obtain written photo use permission from each person in your photographs (for minors or others unable to legally sign for themselves, have the parent or guardian sign). Also, inform all parents or guardians of your intent to provide an integrated outdoor recreation program and obtain their consent. This permission may not be required, but may avoid a misunderstanding.

Using Cooperative Grouping Arrangements Successfully

The importance of social interactions and group affiliation through social support is often understated. "Social support" is the existence and availability of people on whom one can rely for assistance, support, and caring (Johnson *et al.*, 1985). The perception of social support in a group is related generally to academic achievement, persistence to complete challenging tasks under frustrating conditions, academic and career aspirations, resilience in stressful situations, self-reliance and autonomy, a coherent and integrated self-identity, and psychological health and adjustment.

Social support during a group activity can be promoted by cooperatively structuring the goals. A cooperative goal structure specifies the type of interdependence needed among group members and the way in which participants need to relate to each other and to the group leader to accomplish the goal. A number of goal structures are commonly used.

Cooperative goal structure. Participants understand that they can obtain their goal if, and only if, all participants in the group work to achieve the same goal. Participants can be brought together to create a list of factors that favors the snowshoe hare over the cottontail rabbit for winter survival. Given that the goal of the activity is for all students to create this list, the cooperative goal has been reached when all contribute to the list, even if the contribution is fastening the pages of the list together.

Competitive goal structure. Participants perceive that they can obtain their goal if, and only if, other participants fail to obtain their goal. In a competition to determine who can master canoe paddling skills the fastest, one or a select few participants may achieve their goal but it is at the expense of other participants. For every winner, there is a loser.

Individualistic goal structure. Achievement of the goal by one participant is unrelated to the achievement of goals by other participants. For example, participants are asked to quietly complete a worksheet matching adaptations for winter survival to the appropriate animal; completing the worksheet has no bearing upon whether other participants successfully achieve the

Natural challenges inspire cooperative solutions.

activity goal. Participant interaction is minimal because each participant seeks the best personal outcome. The essential idea is to compete against yourself.

The activity leader should consider several factors when deciding which goal structure is appropriate:

1. What are the desired cognitive, social, and affective outcomes for the activity?

2. How does the organization of the physical environment relate to the goal structure? Does the physical environment facilitate participant access to other participants, the group leader, and needed materials?

3. What is the nature and amount of interaction within the group, between group members, and with the instructional materials and equipment?

4. What are your responsibilities as a leader in this situation?

5. How can you tell whether participant behavior is appropriate to the goal structure?

6. How will participant outcomes be evaluated?

7. How much are you enjoying the leadership role in this activity?

When leaders are familiar with all three goal structures, possess the necessary skills to implement them, and have experience working within each, they will probably be good judges of which goal structure is most desirable for specified activities. When leaders do not have past experience with these goal structures, or do not possess the skills necessary to successfully develop them, an informed and free choice cannot occur.

When participants expect the group to achieve a goal, they also expect to have positive interactions with other participants, to share ideas and materials, to get group support for taking risks in thinking and trying out skills, to have every member contribute in some way to achieve the goal, and to divide the labor among the members of the group.

Four factors are important in establishing a cooperative goal structure:

1. Present the goal as a *group goal*.

2. Facilitate and encourage the *sharing of ideas and materials*.

3. Facilitate and encourage the *sharing of labor* when appropriate. It is appropriate for all participants to engage in brainstorming possible goal attainments at the beginning of the activity.

4. *Reward the group* for cooperative completion of a task. All participants should share in successfully achieving the group goal. Emphasize that the *group* has successfully completed the task. Direct most feedback to the group and avoid praising only a few members.

An example may help to clarify the technique in action. Several groups are given the problem of why a row of grapevines was planted on a fence row. Instead of a single solution, the class generates a range of answers in their discussion. Participants suggest that the location of the grapevines on the fence, and who might eat the grapes, may have affected their answers. "How many items can the group locate that would tell us how those grapevines were planted?" A recorder is designated and the participants are encouraged to compare ideas and to have other students verify their suggestions.

During cooperatively goal-structured activities, it is important to define roles and expectations for leaders and participants. The expectations include: (a) participants viewing each other as a major resource; participants are expected to talk with each other and to see what others are doing; (b) the outdoor educator is a catalyst in making suggestions and supplying additional equipment but is not the primary resource; the leader expects participants to rely on each other for ideas and the verification of solutions; and (c) a variety of materials is available rather than a standard set for each participant; sharing materials is expected.

Participants may not know how to work with others during cooperative activities. It is, therefore, important to address the following items to increase participants' abilities to function in groups:

1. Ask participants what skills they will need to cooperate (compete, work individually) successfully. In order to be motivated to learn a skill, participants must understand the need for the skill. If the participant does not suggest the needed skills, the program leader should help participants understand why it is important to acquire the skill.

2. Help participants understand the skill, conceptually and behaviorally. First, behaviors must be identified and placed in proper sequence and in close succession. Demonstrate the skill, describe it step-by-step, and then demonstrate it again. Also identify other participants who can perform the skill successfully.

3. Organize practice situations. Once a skill is understood, behavioral patterns should be practiced until they are mastered.

4. Ensure that each participant receives feedback on how well she is performing the skill. Feedback is necessary to correct errors, identify problems and progress, and compare actual performance with the desired standard. Behavior specific positive feedback (BSPF) may be the single most important factor affecting skill acquisition. The more immediate, specific, and descriptive the feedback, the more it facilitates skill development. Feedback is often quite interesting to a participant and may increase motivation to learn the skill. Dividing participants into cooperative groups, in which the members offer each other feedback on task performance, is often effective.

5. Encourage participants to persevere in practicing the skill. The process of learning most skills involves a period of slow noticeable change in skill proficiency, followed by a period of rapid gain, followed by a plateau in which performance does not increase dramatically.

6. Structure situations in which the skills can be used successfully. Participants will receive reinforcement naturally as they function more effectively in the cooperative goal structures.

7. Require the skills to be used often enough that they become integrated into the participants' behavioral repertoire.

8. Set norms to support the use of these skills. Modeling the skills, rewarding participants who appropriately engage in the skills, and explicitly stating how you expect participants to behave will influence the degree to which participants engage in behavior appropriate to the goal structure.

Prepare Adults as Facilitators

A program leader who assumes a facilitating role is instrumental in determining the success or failure of integrated activities. Facilitation takes two forms:

— Planning and operation of the program, including recruiting participants, structuring activities, and preparing nondisabled peers for the integrated program.

— Modeling appropriate behavior and reinforcing group interactions.

For a group engaged in an outdoor art activity, the leader could interact to:

— *Encourage positive interactions* when they are not occurring. "Mary, I'll bet that Jennifer would like to make vegetable prints with you."

— *Reinforce positive interactions* when they are occurring. "Bill and Jim, you both did a nice job with the environmental mural." Rewarding words should not be provided indiscriminately; they should be given immediately following the desired behavior.

— *Redirect behaviors* if either partner gets off track or behaves inappropriately. A nondisabled partner may become "sloppy" in interactions by becoming autocratic, too laissez faire, or absorbed in a personal project. Or a participant with a disability may wander away from her/ his companion.

— *Step in if a situation is deteriorating.* A participant has a tantrum and may need to be removed for a cooling-off period. The adult leader needs to gauge the seriousness of a problem and move in quickly if it is out of control, or better yet, when it is just beginning to get out of control.

Prepare Trainer Advocates

The use of a trainer advocate (*e.g.*, a volunteer, peer, sibling, or staff member) to assist a participant individually in a vocational setting, as a job coach, has been successfully generalized to recreation and outdoor education settings (Wehman & Schleien, 1981). A trainer advocate encourages cooperation, reinforces positive interactions between peers, facilitates group interactions, and remains unobtrusive.

A trainer advocate may also help resolve problems. The advocate attempts to create a positive atmosphere in which the abilities of the individual are highlighted, and similarities with nondisabled participants are reinforced. The trainer advocate position is temporary because assistance should decrease as participants become socially integrated into the activity.

The trainer advocate acts as an instructor's "tool," helping ensure the normal "flow and rhythm" of the activity. The trainer advocate is a companion and may provide one-on-one assistance to the individual who is disabled. She may provide necessary support to and instill confidence in individuals who have experienced failure or rejection in the past. Schleien and Ray (1988) identified the following responsibilities of a trainer advocate in a community recreation or outdoor education program:

1. Facilitates interpersonal relationships among group members.

2. Physically prompts the participant to perform a task (*e.g.*, gesturing to a person to reach out to touch a tree).

3. Manages problem behaviors if they occur.

4. Analyzes tasks and teaches outdoor education and other leisure/social skills to the participants.

5. Evaluates in an ongoing manner participant involvement in the outdoor education program.

6. Provides transportation assistance to and from the outdoor education site.

7. Assists participants during toileting, dressing, grooming, and other self-care skills.

8. Assists with mobility throughout the program (*e.g.*, pushing a wheelchair, walking beside participants, and providing needed physical support).

9. Provides other assistance as determined by parents, teachers, care providers, and outdoor education staff.

10. Serves as the link between a participant who is disabled and the outdoor educator.

A trainer advocate must be familiar with many techniques and procedures to be effective. She should be a proficient observer to determine the assistance necessary at a particular time. The techniques include:

Task analysis. Many professionals and researchers (Dattilo & Murphy, 1991; Wehman & Schleien, 1981; Wuerch & Voeltz, 1982) have supported the use of task analysis in teaching recreation and outdoor education skills to individuals with disabilities. By depicting the steps of an activity that are easily teachable and observable, task analysis serves as an assessment tool of skill proficiency; it also individualizes a program, allowing for adaptations based on a participant's needs and abilities. Task analysis provides a teaching sequence that can be used consistently by other outdoor educators or naturalists. A sample task analysis for "fishing" could include the following six steps:

1. Bait hook.

2. Cast fishing line into body of water.

3. Watch bobber floating on water's surface.

4. When bobber disappears beneath the surface, jerk rod toward body to hook fish.

5. Reel in line.

6. Remove fish (or seaweed) from hook.

Instructional cue hierarchy and prompting system. Cues and prompts are important parts of instructional programs that attempt to elicit behaviors before they are mastered. Prompts (usually arranged in a hierarchy of least-to-most intrusive) help foster new behaviors or correct undesirable ones; they may include physical guidance, modeling appropriate behaviors, gestures, and verbal direction. A desirable outcome of instruction through outdoor education materials is to have instructional cues or prompts become natural environmental cues that elicit appropriate and independent behavior.

Reinforcement. Because individuals with disabilities seldom find many activities enjoyable during early training sessions, a reinforcement component is usually included. Reinforcement consists of delivering desirable events, consequences, or objects to an individual immediately following the occurrence of an appropriate response. The strength of reinforcement lies in immediate delivery. Effective reinforcers, often highly individualized, increase the likelihood that the desired response will reoccur. Common and effective reinforcers are person-specific and may include food, praise, attention, materials and activities that are reactive in nature, and access to favorite outdoor education materials (Dattilo & Murphy, 1987; Wehman & Schleien, 1981). The following list identifies the appropriate times for a trainer advocate to reinforce an individual or group:

1. To encourage individuals in small groups to stay close to each other throughout the activity.

2. To encourage participants to talk with each another when solving problems and working cooperatively.

3. To provide positive feedback when the group works well together.

4. To encourage participants to take turns.

5. To encourage participants to coordinate their efforts within the group.

6. When inappropriate behaviors are exhibited during the program, to speak with participants shortly after the behavior occurs.

7. To provide assistance if the participants appear to be experiencing difficulty but remain on the sidelines.

Several methods can be used to recruit and retain trainer advocates:

1.   Have a job description that is well defined and orderly. A job description outlines specific responsibilities and expectations, including days and hours needed, special skills required, *etc.*

2.   Match skills and interests of the trainer advocate to a participant's skills and interests if possible.

3.   Inform the trainer advocate about an individual's particular disabilities, special needs, strengths, and personal preferences.

4.   Evaluate the program (and the trainer advocate's performance) at the end of the program.

5.   Have the trainer advocate evaluate the outdoor education program and personal performance.

The amount of preparation required by a trainer advocate depends on the program, the disability of the individual or individuals, and the nature of the group. Training could include such information as:

— Goals and objectives of the program.

— Characteristics of persons with disabilities from a functional standpoint.

— Rationale for and benefits of integrated outdoor education programs.

— Information on particular disabilities that will be encountered (could be provided by parents, a member of an advocacy group, a care provider, or teacher).

— Policies and procedures of the program, including emergency procedures.

— Information particular to the individual to be integrated (information from parents, care providers, or teachers).

— Site orientation.

— Evaluation of programs.

— Methods to achieve successful integrated programs, including observation techniques, reinforcement techniques, task analysis, and cooperative grouping arrangements.

A trainer advocate in an outdoor education setting: A case study

SETTING: *Belwin Outdoor Education Laboratory.*

PARTICIPANTS: *Eight third-grade students [seven from regular education classrooms, and one (Suzi) who was diagnosed with autism]; one special education teacher; one regular education teacher; one naturalist; and a classroom teacher who served as Suzi's trainer advocate.*

PROGRAM: *The students are observing a decaying log. The naturalist asks students why the log is falling apart. Various responses are given by the students. The naturalist explains how insects, fungus, and tiny bugs are chewing the log apart. The students explore the log. Suzi begins to eat pieces of the log. The trainer advocate physically removes Suzi's hand to redirect her attention away from this inappropriate behavior. A regular education student shows Suzi a section of the log. The trainer advocate reinforces the interaction by saying, "Joey, that was nice of you to share what you found with Suzi; Suzi, can you find something to share with Joey?" Suzi locates a leaf with holes in it and shows it to Joey. She tells him that bugs ate the holes in the leaf. The trainer advocate reinforces Suzi by saying, "Suzi, that was very nice of you to find something interesting to show to Joey."*

The naturalist directs the students' attention to a deer print on the trail. All the students follow the naturalist. Suzi reaches for Tina (a regular education student) and pulls her hair. Tina doesn't say anything. The trainer advocate intervenes and explains to Suzi, "It is not nice to pull Tina's hair." She tells Tina, "Tina, you don't have to let Suzi pull your hair; you can tell her to stop it because you don't like it."

Environmental Analysis Approach:
Assessing People, Not "Disabilities"

During the planning and development of an integrated outdoor education program, specific modifications can be made to enhance participation by persons with disabilities. To promote social integration, the outdoor educator, in collaboration with other key personnel, should complete an *Environmental Analysis Inventory* (Certo, Schleien & Hunter, 1983; Schleien & Ray, 1988).

The inventory provides the outdoor educator, and others responsible for designing a program, with a systematic approach to promoting the successful involvement of all participants. Using the inventory helps heighten awareness and increase the level of sensitivity of all persons involved in the programming process.

The inventory begins when specific needs or concerns regarding a participant are identified. The outdoor educator should ask several questions to assure that the "participant-program match" is appropriate. Is this targeted activity consistent with the participant's needs, strengths, and preferences? Are adaptations available that could promote a successful experience for the participant with special needs?

The *Environmental Analysis Inventory* has several distinct advantages over more traditional, "fly-by-the-seat-of-your-pants" approaches:

1. It is a step-by-step procedural process to integrate persons into outdoor education and other community recreation programs.

2. It is an individualized approach that addresses the personal needs of staff members.

3. It provides useful information to people who are responsible for planning and facilitating an outdoor education experience and it aids current and future programming.

4. It relates the outdoor education experience to nondisabled persons to enhance appropriateness and functionality for the participant who is disabled.

Readers will find a more comprehensive discussion of how to implement an *Environmental Analysis Inventory* of outdoor education programs in the bibliography. Based on this information, companionship training, cooperative grouping arrangements, trainer advocacy, and/or behavioral procedures can be incorporated into the integrated outdoor education or wilderness adventure program.

Cross-country skiing on a sit-ski.

Chapter Five

PROGRAM ADAPTATIONS FOR SUCCESSFUL INTEGRATION

Sometimes people with disabilities have problems seeing (blindness), hearing (deafness), thinking (mental retardation), manipulating objects and moving around (physical impairment), or socializing (social maladjustment). We have many specific names for disabilities: cerebral palsy, Down syndrome, cystic fibrosis, retinal detachment, and epilepsy; but they are just names. A disability is relative to the demands of the environment in which the individual is attempting to function. Disabilities and labels tell us little about how an individual with an impairment functions as a person. The focus of this chapter is not on the disability, but on functional adaptations the person needs for learning, recreating, and forming relationships. We are concerned with how activities can be made more accessible, more tolerant of limitations in skills, and more accepting of partial participation by people with disabilities.

An *adaptation* is a change in a standard component of an activity. These changes may include the materials and equipment used, the manner in which they are manipulated, or the environment in which the activity takes place (Wehman & Schleien, 1981). Adaptations can enable, and even enhance, a participant's performance in an activity, including outdoor education and adventure programming. Socialization, self-sufficiency, motor development, and enjoyment can also be facilitated. Ultimately, the acquisition of new physical, recreation, and social skills leads to increased opportunities for friendship and a more normalized lifestyle.

When functional adaptations are made, participants with disabilities see, hear, think, move around, communicate, and socialize more ably. Participants without disabilities may be able to learn more effectively, too. After all, individuals without disabilities or labels also have problems "hearing" (listening to directions), "thinking" (sequencing project elements), "seeing" (following printed directions), and "moving and manipulating objects" (moving too far too fast).

A number of strategies for successful and appropriate adaptations are discussed in this chapter, including general guidelines, different types of adaptations, and practical tips. Each type of outdoor education or adventure program requires general adaptations and program-specific ones. It is impossible to describe every possible outdoor program adaptation; instead, we describe general adaptations that will help make outdoor program integration a reality. Think of this chapter as attempting to teach programmers how to catch fish for themselves, as opposed to us catching a fish for each reader. Adaptations for canoeing serve as an example of the creative possibilities.

Guidelines for Adapting Activities

Consistent with the principle of normalization, all persons should participate in activities in as normal a manner as feasible. Therefore, it is necessary to carefully analyze the environment before changes are made in an activity. When adaptations are made appropriately, the perceived differences between participants with and without disabilities are minimized. The following guidelines are helpful in assisting program leaders install successful and appropriate adaptations.

1. *Adapt only when necessary.* Unfortunately, many people make adaptations without considering a person's actual needs. An activity leader will use a modification because it was purchased or because she is familiar with its application. A naturalist had all of her students using adapted tools during a pond study, even though only one student needed them. Do

not overlook the ability level of the participant; a simplified version of an activity may not be required.

By starting with a thorough analysis of the planned activity, the leader can pinpoint skills required for successful participation. Following the activity analysis, the participants' abilities to perform are assessed. Adapt only when necessary!

2. *View adaptations as temporary and transitional.* Many people view adaptations as a "fix" or a support to allow people with disabilities to participate equally. Unfortunately, adaptations are usually a poor substitute for the real thing. They may be quite useful in helping to develop basic confidence and skills; however, whenever possible, program leaders must work toward normalizing the intended activity rather than considering the adaptation sufficient. For example, if a program leader wants to promote canoeing, she may start by offering simple canoe lessons in an indoor swimming pool environment. The pool environment allows greater control and comfort in helping to develop base skills. However, this environment is no substitute for canoeing outdoors. As soon as participants have mastered the "adaptation" of the indoor pool environment, they should be "graduated" to a more normalized setting for canoeing–a lake or river.

3. *Adapt on an individual basis.* Many practitioners pay "lip service" to the idea that people with disabilities function at different levels, but then they treat them all the same in practice. Treat all participants as individuals, making special arrangements on an individual basis. In a nontraditional science class studying aerodynamics, 12 students with motor problems were observed tossing light-weight Nerf frisbees, yet only two did not have the minimum eye-hand coordination needed to throw a standard, plastic frisbee, which performs better outdoors. When asked why all were using the modified equipment, the science teacher responded, "Well, we recently purchased a carton of Nerf frisbees for the science program. Also it's too dangerous for the two students without the requisite coordination to play with a hard frisbee." It apparently did not matter to her that 10 students never received instruction commensurate with their ability levels.

The teacher should have individualized the modification so that only the two for whom it was absolutely necessary (and possibly two additional students for integration purposes) used the Nerf frisbees.

4. *Adapt for normalization.* If an individual requires a modification, keep it as close to the standard version as possible. Unnecessarily exaggerated adaptations such as Nerf frisbees versus plastic ones make a participant stand out. Making other participants more aware of differences rather than similarities does not promote social integration.

5. *Adapt for availability.* Often an individual becomes accustomed to using adapted equipment or materials in a "training" environment, but these modifications are not found or readily available in "non-training" settings. For example, a person who learns to fish using an adapted rod and reel may not always have access to these special materials. Hence, it would be more practical to teach the individual how to use a commercially available rod and reel, making fishing accessible in any pond or lake. Admittedly, elaborate and expensive devices, such as adapted fishing piers, are necessary for persons with more severe disabilities and should be employed when available. It is the activity leader's responsibility to consider these factors when making adaptation decisions.

Adaptations in Outdoor Education and High Adventure Programs

Relatively few disabling conditions prohibit participation in outdoor recreation (see Chapter 3). Most people with disabilities can participate in canoeing, kayaking, rafting, or dog sledding, provided careful attention is given to developing adaptations that help bridge the gap beween their needs and the demands of the activity or environment.

Adaptations can be categorized into five basic types. These include:

1. *Material adaptations* (e.g., to gather seeds, use a large plastic pail instead of a small dish).

2. *Procedural and rule adaptations* (e.g., to gather pond samples, work from a dock rather than the edge of a pond, and have everyone wear personal flotation devices such as lifejackets).

3. *Skill sequence adaptations* (e.g., before a snowshoe hike in the woods, put on the snowshoes indoors).

4. *Environmental modifications* (e.g., make walking paths hard surfaced rather than graveled).

5. *Lead-up activities* (e.g., learn to paddle in a swimming pool before canoeing outdoors).

Partial Participation

In addition to changing the activity or environment, accept that people with varying abilities may participate only partially. This participation, although it may look different, is better than no participation at all. Remember, it is only important that an individual participate to her or his maximum potential. Partial participation is enhanced by assistance from nondisabled peers (including trainer advocates and companions), cooperative grouping arrangements, and learning activities.

The number of combinations of people, activities, and environments are endless. Instead of listing the thousands of possible conditions programmers may face, provided below is a system for categorizing some of the most common situations according to an individual's ability to function within that area. For example, persons with spinal cord injuries, multiple sclerosis, cerebral palsy, and deafness may all be affected by poor balance. Rather than consider the ramifications of this for each disability type, this section addresses the functional problems associated with poor balance and provides a framework for developing adaptations that address poor balance.

Functional Impairments

A *functional impairment*, by definition, is the inability or decreased ability to perform a task, activity, or function without adaptation or assistance. In this context, a person with a disability is not necessarily disabled in every function. The converse is also true; not every nondisabled person is able to perform every function without some assistance. A key to making an integrated outdoor program work is the ability of staff members to use each person's strengths and to encourage cooperative relationships that alleviate the effects of a disability.

Eleven major functional activity areas have been selected in two major categories—physical and cognitive. A few functional activities could appear in either grouping (e.g., activities of daily living and communication/language).

Physical disabilities typically affect only physical abilities and characteristics, including:

— Activities of daily living.

— Balance.

— Buoyancy.

— Circulation.

— Sensation.

— Motor control.

— Fatigue.

— Diet.

Cognitive disabilities affect intellectual and emotional characteristics, including:

— Judgment.

— Memory loss.

— Communication/language.

Staff of integrated programs must know the specifics of functional impairments and how to make adaptations. The benefits are:

— Enhanced social integration.

— Increased participation by persons with disabling conditions.

— Increased safety.

— Improved ability to solve problems that arise.

— Reduction of stereotypic thinking.

Importance of Common Sense

Staff members of mixed-ability groups continuously take calculated risks to provide the safest options for the greatest gains in personal growth. The extent of adaptation should be governed by common sense. If a staff member is in doubt, she should test it under safe circumstances to determine the worst possible danger. If the tester is not satisfied that the adaptation is safe, she should reject it. Some individuals have recommended canoe seat belts for individuals with balance problems—but what happens when the canoe overturns, possibly trapping the person underwater? Common sense dictates that safety risks of a seat belt nullify its use.

About Adaptations

Every important adaptation starts with the "equipment" between the ears of the staff and the participants. Each individual's conditions and situations are unique; adaptations to increase participation in an event are also unique. Flexibility and creativity are crucial to integrating people with and without disabilities in a mixed-ability program.

Many people believe that, by making a few mechanical adaptations, they can help a person with a disability perform a function as well as a nondisabled person. This usually is not the case, particularly outdoors. Most physical adaptations suggested here will improve a person's efficiency in a given function, but they seldom, if ever, will make that person as proficient at a given task as one who is not disabled.

What may work for one person may not work for another, even though the situation may seem to be the same. *The importance of communication and feedback between staff and participants cannot be understated.* Staff members should always begin a major activity by asking the person with a disability what she thinks is the best option for adapting a situation to increase participation.

NOTE: The information and practices described throughout the remainder of the chapter should be considered introductory and basic. We strongly urge the outdoor educator or trip leader to consult with physicians and reference materials to fully understand the technical information related to specific disabilities and functional impairments. The information here is not intended for unquestioned adoption by any program and cannot be used indiscriminately. It should be adapted to the needs of specific programs and individuals.

The medical and personal care practices were developed and adapted from several sources (see the bibliography). Also, we consulted with physicians, physical therapists, registered nurses, certified therapeutic recreation specialists, outdoor professionals, and other health care professionals. We especially thank Kelly Cain, Holly Church, Howard Cohen, Deb Erdmann, Wayne Freimund, Jay Johnson, Jeanne Kogl, Jane Link, Becky Lucas, Craig Luedemann, Don Mitchell, Robin Monahan, Carol Perry, Kevin Proescholdt, Paul Schurke, Bill Simpson, Camp Sunrise, Patti Thurber, and William Waring for their assistance.

Finally, many of these practices and strategies have been developed, field-tested, and/or modified by Wilderness Inquiry *over 15 years of field experiences. Neither the publisher nor the authors endorse these*

> *practices in any formal manner or accept responsibility for their adoption. The interpretation and application of these practices are at the discretion and responsibility of the reader.*

Activities of Daily Living

Activities of daily living (ADLs) are normal day-to-day tasks that everyone performs to function—eating, dressing, toileting, and personal hygiene. In an outdoor environment, daily group schedules should be discussed and agreed upon, as much as possible, at the beginning of the day or activity to allow time for adjustment to individual needs.

Site Access

Although many outdoor environments cannot be manipulated to enhance accessibility, groups that include persons with mobility impairments should keep accessibility in mind when selecting program areas or campsites. Sandy, rocky, or sloped environments are not conducive to active participation by people who use wheelchairs. However, the reality of outdoor activities may necessitate using such an environment in a pinch.

Remind participants who do not use wheelchairs to be alert to the need for accessibility. Ambulatory people may absent-mindedly place a pack or pile of equipment across an otherwise accessible pathway, interfering with access to the activity, personal packs, cooking area, tents, or latrine areas. Establish a group policy to make accessibility a priority. Offer the most accessible environments (e.g., tent sites) to people with the greatest mobility impairments.

Toileting

The issues of privacy, minimum impact camping, and accessibility to the toilet sometimes conflict. Toileting issues should be discussed openly during program screening and during the activity. Persons who need assistance to get to a latrine, to clean up, or in actual elimination functions are often apprehensive about toileting. Persons who lack sensation and muscle control below the waist are likely to experience occasional or regular incontinence (i.e., inability to retain natural evacuations), often as the result of a high-fiber diet. Staff members must always be sensitive to the social issues involved with toileting.

Many people who have spinal cord injuries or other conditions that affect muscle control and/or sensation below the waist routinely require suppositories, digital stimulation, and/or use of laxatives to defecate; this is referred to as a bowel program (BP). Many participants can independently follow the program if they have a stable toilet area.

Standard equipment for areas without restrooms includes a portable toilet resembling a folding chair with a toilet seat. Most people find these chairs to be adequate, allowing them to comfortably perform toileting functions. In certain outdoor areas there are primitive latrines with box toilets, which should be used as much as possible. If access to established latrines is a problem, staff members should set up the portable toilet in an appropriate place. A tarp can be rigged to offer a degree of privacy, and all human waste can be removed and disposed of in an ecologically sound latrine. A participant who needs assistance with suppositories or cleaning generally must be accompanied by a personal care attendant. Minimum impact camping practices should not be compromised when it comes to toileting issues.

Colostomies. Some people have had their colons re-routed so that feces come out in a small bag attached to their abdomen. The staff should be aware of the possibility of leakage. Caution is advised when transferring a person with a colostomy to avoid pulling or placing undue pressure on the bag.

Effects of food and water. Constipation and/or diarrhea are common experiences during wilderness trips, especially during the first few days. These conditions are due to an adjustment to the drinking water or the general diet. Neither condition is a cause for great concern unless it continues for more than three days, but make sure participants consume large amounts of water.

Frequent or urgent urination. People who lack sensation or muscle control below the waist are likely to have some difficulty controlling urination. People who need to urinate frequently may be well advised to bring a urinal—especially during periods in a canoe or sailboat when repeated stopping is impractical.

Catheters. Some people use a catheter to control urination. There are two types: in-dwelling and external. Females and some males use in-dwelling catheters, which consist of a tube inserted through the urethra into the bladder. It is held in place by a special bulb that is inflated with sterile water inside the bladder. The tube exits the urethra, follows down the leg, and attaches to a bag, which is usually secured around the ankle.

If a person cannot maintain the in-dwelling catheter, she can have an attendant along. Although most outdoor staff members are not required to insert, sterilize, or otherwise maintain catheters, they should be familiar enough with them to assist in an emergency. People who use in-dwelling catheters are susceptible to bladder and urinary tract infections; sterility is very important.

The external catheter, or condom catheter, consists of a condom with a tube in the end of it. The tube is attached to a leg bag (Figure 5.1). Condom catheters are easier to use because they attach easily and reduce the risk of bladder infections; however, sometimes they must be glued or taped on. Both types of catheters have drawbacks in outdoor environments. Condom catheters can be pulled off during transferring, causing mess and embarrassment. Internal catheters can be pulled out if caution is

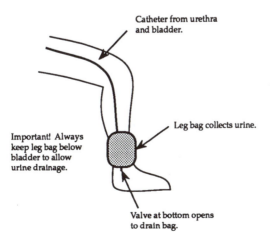

Figure 5.1. External catheter.

not exercised during transfers. With either type, remember that it is important to keep the urine bag below the level of the bladder to prevent urine from flowing back into the bladder and increasing the chances for infection. Leg bags should be emptied frequently.

Eating

Some people who are severely affected by cerebral palsy, head injury, or stroke, or who have upper limb limitations, may need assistance to eat. In some cases, it is simply a matter of having someone assist in getting food from the bowl to the mouth, a task that can be rotated among group members. As an integration technique, it is often beneficial to assign participants who are less capable at helping in other program activities to assist those who need help eating. But make certain that someone willingly helps out—otherwise the person who needs assistance may sit with a full bowl and no way to eat.

People who have spasticity in their jaws or above-normal tongue movements may need to have food cut up into small pieces. Their eating may be quite labored, and on occasion, unpleasant to watch due to difficulty in keeping food in their mouths. Under these circumstances, it is best not to make them laugh, cough, or otherwise disrupt their eating behaviors.

IMPORTANT: If providing assistance for eating, never "bird feed" or tip back the head of a person who has difficulty sucking or swallowing. Keep the head erect to avoid choking.

Adapted eating aids are available, including straws, deep cups with big handles, bent spoons for easier gripping, or taping a spoon handle to the hand of a person with a weak grip. Straws allow people to be independent in drinking fluids. Cups and glasses with tall sides for straws and better gripping are other important adaptations. Many agencies have them in stock, but most people who use such devices should be encouraged to bring their own from home. Check to make sure participants have the devices needed.

A useful adaptation for many people is simply to use a board, pack, or other device that can serve as a table or platform upon which to balance a bowl. Many individuals who can eat independently at a table have difficulty both holding dishes in their laps and getting the food to their mouths; a table can make a big difference.

Other Daily Living Activities

Some people also require assistance in dressing, brushing their teeth, *etc.* If a person needs significant assistance (*e.g.*, can perform less than 50 percent of the activities independently), it is recommended that she or he bring a personal care attendant along. Otherwise, staff members and other participants can help, especially if the atmosphere is one of mutual assistance.

Some people develop an attitude of "getting grubby" while on trail, especially if cleaning themselves is difficult due to impaired mobility. Staff members should stress the importance of regular washing, teeth brushing, etc., and make it clear to everyone that they will assist in those functions when necessary.

Balance

A lack of balance is a common problem among many people with disabilities. Poor balance may be caused by loss of muscle function, brain damage, improperly functioning cochlea (inner ear), or lack of sensation. Identifying balance problems is usually a matter of observation or of asking the individual. People who have spent little time outdoors may not know how their balance will be in certain circumstances. Some may insist that their balance and mobility are good, but they are used to pavement and accessible buildings. Can they travel up a hill unassisted or walk along a river bank? Have they ever walked in a freshly plowed field? In most cases, resolving balance problems involves common sense.

Land Balance

Most terrain is not flat and smooth like a sidewalk. Anyone can fall and twist an ankle, break an arm, or hit his head. Staff members must allow people with balance problems the time to ambulate safely. The staff should reinforce the common sense concept of being careful. In some cases, particularly among people who have had closed head injuries, it may be best for a participant with poor balance to wear a helmet when crossing a rough trail or off-trail area.

Fires. People who are likely to trip and fall into a fire should be requested to limit their activity to outside "falling" distance of the fire. Some people, once stabilized, can cook and perform other functions around a fire. When on any kind of a slope, persons using wheelchairs should lock and/or block their wheels around fires. Make sure the person will not slide out of a wheelchair and into the fire.

Hazardous terrain. Steep trails; lake, river, and ocean shores; and other potentially hazardous terrain always should be approached with caution. Most people are naturally cautious around such areas, but some will not seem to notice or care (see section on judgment). If necessary, staff members must be prepared to escort or carry participants with balance problems around hazardous places.

Portages. Portaging is carrying canoes or small boats across land to get from one water body to another, or to get from a parking lot or other land area to a water body. It is an activity well suited to the goals of team building and the development of cooperative relationships. In addition to innate capability, balance on a portage is determined by the trail, the load a person is carrying (if any), and such situational factors as fatigue or rain.

It is best to start slow and easy on portages. Encourage persons with questionable balance to start by carrying light, unbreakable items that may pad a fall, such as life jackets, extra sleeping bags, cushions, etc. Do not expect persons with questionable balance to carry packs, canoes, kayaks, or other heavy items until they have proven that they can negotiate the terrain safely. If the trail appears to be more than the person can negotiate alone, staff members should suggest a team effort, such as holding on to someone's arm (possibly two, one on each arm) for additional support. In these situations, encourage the formation of teams to safely assist each other. Some participants can serve as guides while others are carriers and stabilizers. (See Chapter 4.)

Time is an important consideration during portages. Provide people with balance or mobility impairments ample time to cross a trail (start them out first, after the trail has been scouted to ensure no steep cliffs or other hazards). Staff members should try to allow enough time for everyone to cross the trail as independently as possible. However, if it is late in the day, or if everyone else is waiting around, it may be best to offer assistance. Use discretion and always ask the people involved.

Tents. People with poor balance may have difficulty getting in and out of tents—especially when bugs are biting! Attaching a short teather to a zipper head makes the zipper much easier to use. Provide instruction on how to keep dirt, rain, and bugs out.

Mobility-enhancing Land Devices

Canes. Quad canes are the best walking aids for participation in the outdoors. They do not poke through moss, mud, or sand. Normal canes can also be helpful on hard terrain. Participants should fit their crutches with tough, non-skid tips.

Wheelchairs. Wheelchairs can be functional outdoors. Lightweight sports chairs work best. The two major factors in determining the utility of wheelchairs on a trip are the type of terrain and the ability of the user.

Terrain conditions vary from one outdoor area to the next, but without pavement, wheelchair users lose some independence and mobility. Unless staff members are certain that no impassable obstructions exist, everyone who uses a wheelchair should be prepared to be carried (see Chapter 3).

User ability also varies. Although they will still require assistance on most outdoor excursions, active persons with good upper body strength can do well in a wheelchair. Determine a participant's ability before the outdoor program, either by direct observation or by telephone confirmation. The staff should know the terrain in advance and prepare wheelchair users for likely consequences. Wheelchairs may be cumbersome or heavy. Persons with little upper body strength or function are less likely to make productive use of a wheelchair. Even so, most people who use wheelchairs prefer to bring them; try to accommodate these needs. As a specific example, carrying wheelchairs in canoes is described in Figures 5.2 and 5.3.

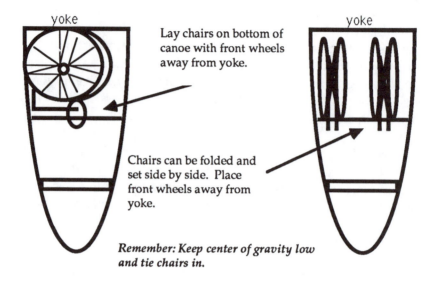

yoke

Lay chairs on bottom of
canoe with front wheels
away from yoke.

Chairs can be folded and
set side by side. Place
front wheels away from
yoke.

yoke

*Remember: Keep center of gravity low
and tie chairs in.*

*Figure 5.2. Loading a folding wheelchair into a
canoe. Most wheelchairs can be safely loaded in the mid-
section.*

Tips for loading wheelchairs in canoes:

— Budget extra space in the canoe to accommodate chairs.

— Extra flotation may be necessary in some canoes loaded
with wheelchairs. To be safe, test under actual conditions.

— Tie straps are important to prevent the wheelchair from
being lost if the canoe capsizes. The added difficulty of a
wheelchair dangling upside down in the water during a
rescue also should be considered. Test tie-in arrangements to make sure that no one will be trapped by the
rigging. Be prepared to cut the tie and release the wheelchair quickly in an emergency.

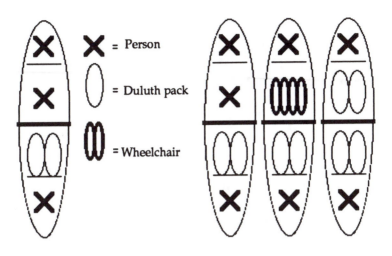

Figure 5.3. Typical loading arrangement for group of 10 people (two people per #4 personal Duluth pack).

— Some people gain considerable independence transferring from wheelchair to canoe by using transfer boards. These boards also can double as a table for people who need a stable platform while eating.

Lawn chairs. To reduce weight, lawn chairs can sometimes be substituted for wheelchairs, especially for people who lack the upper body strength to use their wheelchairs in rugged terrain. However, the lawn chair may not provide the degree of comfort and support required. People who lack sensation are more likely to get pressure sores from sitting in a lawn chair for prolonged periods. For this reason, agencies may restrict the use of lawn chairs to those individuals who have full sensation (*i.e.*, primarily people who are severely affected by cerebral palsy). Substituting a lawn chair for a wheelchair usually sacrifices any independent mobility—unless the person is able and willing to crawl. Staff members should be sensitive to a person's desire to bring a wheelchair, even if it will be of little use.

Walkers. Sometimes walkers provide assistance. Wheels should be removed and replaced with rugged crutch tips. A participant may not be able to use a walker to cross a trail independently, but it can greatly increase independence in an outdoor activity area.

Water Balance

Poor balance in a canoe or kayak must be approached cautiously. Special attention should be given to:

— Center of gravity.

— Lateral (left and right) motion.

— Forward and backward motion.

Center of gravity. Every canoe or kayak is more stable when the center of gravity is kept low, which is achieved by keeping the weight close to the keel (middle of the bottom of the watercraft). However, there is a trade-off between paddling efficiency and a low center of gravity. Generally persons with poor balance should use a watercraft with a low center of gravity. Seat pads and cushions raise the center of gravity.

Depending on the canoe design, the center of gravity can be reduced by lowering the seat (Figure 5.4). Seat adaptations are simple to make. Lowering the seat enhances stability but may diminish paddling efficiency. The best range is usually from three to six inches below the gunwale. On an aluminum canoe lowering the seat is easy (Figure 5.5):

The center of gravity is determined by the distance between the person's body and the keel of the canoe. Less distance means greater stability. Most canoe seats are too high: lower is better.

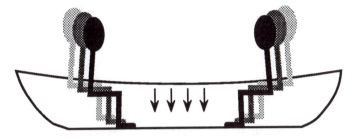

Figure 5.4. Lowering the seat of a canoe to enhance balance.

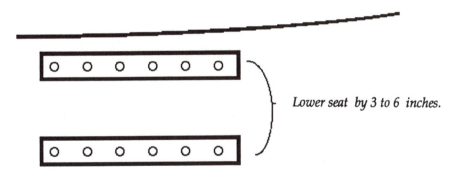

Lower seat by 3 to 6 inches.

Figure 5.5. Lowering seat in an aluminum canoe.

— Drill out the factory rivets.

— Drill new holes several inches below the original placement.

— Re-rivet the seat in the new holes.

— Patch the old holes with silicon sealer (or duct tape).

When three people are in a canoe, the person in the middle—the "duffer"—has an important role in keeping the canoe stable, because the duffer's center of gravity is low. Riding in the middle of a canoe is not as easy as one may think. With some simple adjustments, the ride can be made tolerable, however. Backboards, cushioning, and elevating the knees enhance comfort and stability. Boat cushions are durable seats that double as floating aids or campfire chairs.

Lateral (left and right) body motion. Most persons with poor balance are vulnerable to unexpected lateral motion in a canoe or kayak. Often, the individual is unable to recover from a tilt due to dysfunctional back, trunk, and/or stomach muscles, or because of a poor sense of when one is upright. Paddlers with disabilities must be more cautious in wind and waves. In choppy water, they must repeatedly stop paddling to grab the gunwales (sides of the canoe) to stabilize themselves. For some, the problem can be resolved by wedging sleeping bags or other soft items between the body and the sides of the canoe or kayak.

WARNING: Do not use any device that inhibits easy escape from a canoe, kayak, raft, or sailboat in the event of a tip. Test all devices and arrangements before trusting someone's life to them. Never use chest or seat belts in a canoe, kayak, raft, or boat.

Forward and backward body motion. Backward motion can be reduced or eliminated with the use of adaptations; reducing forward motion is more difficult. Many people with poor balance are prone to sliding off the front of a slick aluminum canoe seat, especially those who cannot brace themselves with their feet due to paralysis. A sheet of *Dycem*, insulite, or other non-skid material can be sandwiched between a person's cushion and the seat to reduce forward slide. Use of non-slip materials on the seat backrest helps reduce sliding. When combined with the elevated knee technique, a backrest with a non-slip surface is an effective aid in most canoeing or kayaking situations. Other options to reduce forward and backward sliding on the seat include:

BACKRESTS. A number of people have developed their own "director's chair" backrests from metal, wood, or PVC tubing. Many agencies stock a clip-on plastic canoe seat backrest made by the *Coleman Company*, which works well for some people.

If the user has no sensation in the lower back, the *Coleman* seat (and most others) should be padded with insulite or other material. People underestimate skin abrasions that can occur when a person is leaning into a seat while paddling. Life jackets should never be relied upon to provide sufficient padding; they move about too easily and expose the skin.

Backboards also are useful, especially when it is possible to wedge them between the seat and the structure of the canoe or kayak. Remember to pad backboards for people without sensation. When backboards are placed across the arm rests of a wheelchair, they double as tables, enhancing the capabilities of people with limited arm function to eat, cut, etc.

SLING SEAT. Wilderness Inquiry developed this adjustable canoe seat to enhance comfort and stability. Consisting of a mesh fabric stretched across aluminum tubing, the "Sling Seat" is suspended from the gunwales by four straps. The length of these straps is adjustable to raise or lower the entire seat or to tip the seat forward or backward.

The Sling Seat is cut large enough to accommodate most pads and cushions. A backboard is inserted in a pocket to protect the back of the paddler from the thwart (crossbar) or the stern plate (back of the canoe). (This board also doubles as a table when laid across wheelchair arm rests.) The straps are secured by "S" hooks that fit into holes drilled into the gunwale of the canoe. Proper padding and cushioning must be used with the Sling Seat for people who lack sensation.

Elevating the knees. Wheelchair racers gain stability by elevating their knees. This technique is modified to increase stability for canoeists, kayakers, and sailors, as well. Raising the knees above the pelvis helps reduce or eliminate forward slide by stabilizing the paddler's legs and pelvis in a position that uses gravity to counteract forward slipping (Figure 5.6).

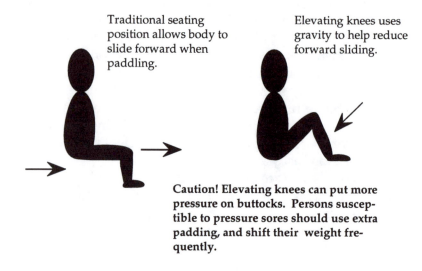

Traditional seating position allows body to slide forward when paddling.

Elevating knees uses gravity to help reduce forward sliding.

Caution! Elevating knees can put more pressure on buttocks. Persons susceptible to pressure sores should use extra padding, and shift their weight frequently.

Figure 5.6. Elevating one's knees in a canoe.

How high the knees should be raised depends on the length of a person's legs and general level of balance. Usually, 3-4 inches is optimal, but experiment to ascertain the most comfortable and efficient position for each person. Legs can be elevated by any number of adaptations:

1. A well-padded dowel rod or broomstick across the gunwales. Notch the ends of the dowel to keep it from sliding back and forth on the gunwale. The best and easiest padding is an insulite sleeping pad rolled and tied or taped around the dowel.

2. A bungee cord hooked into holes drilled into the gunwale. Be sure to pad the cord well.

3. Soft packs, sleeping bags, and other soft items can be wedged into place.

CAUTION: *At least four safety issues must be considered when elevating a person's knees:*

1. Elevating the knees puts additional weight on the buttocks, causing the bony prominences (ishial tuberosites) to put pressure on the skin. This may cause pressure sores. Pad extra well, conduct frequent weight shifts, and check for sores.

2. When legs are elevated, catheter drainage may be diminished or stopped, especially if the drainage bag is hooked to the leg. Do not elevate knees too high or the bladder will not drain properly. An alternative is to detach the urine bag from the leg and allow it to come out the pants' fly to rest on the floor of the canoe or kayak.

3. Pressure sores may occur under the knees. Pad the area extra well.

4. Blood flow to the lower legs may be diminished. Elevate the person's feet occasionally.

Buoyancy

The single greatest danger of water-based outdoor activities is drowning. Each year, thousands of people drown in our lakes, rivers, and oceans. In most cases, these deaths could have been avoided. Many people overestimate their ability to swim and to survive in water. Agencies should require each person (staff members included) to wear life jackets at all times on the water (American National Red Cross, 1977). This simple policy probably does more to prevent accidental death than any other.

Different body types float differently. Muscle and bone are less buoyant than fat, a primary difference between "sinkers" and "floaters." Fat is also a better insulator against cold, which is why sea mammals have blubber and other fatty tissues. Persons with disabling conditions float differently, too, which is related to the density of fat, bone, and muscle or the degree of lung capacity. All persons participating in water-related activities should test their life jackets before an emergency arises.

Adapting a canoe with a Wilderness Inquiry sling seat.

Paralyzed limbs. Paralyzed and atrophied limbs tend to sink. Persons with spinal cord injuries or paralysis should check their life jackets to make sure they float properly. Individuals with hemiplegia may tend to float on one side and have difficulty turning over.

Spasticity. People with cerebral palsy and other disabilities that cause a high degree of spasticity in the limbs are at a disadvantage in the water. First, they tend to have little body fat, and consequently are "sinkers." Second, in many cases, spasticity is increased when they encounter cold water. Persons who are spastic may "freeze" into a ball or arch their backs if they go into the water. Often, there is a tendency for the arms to contract around the life jacket, sometimes causing the jacket to twist or shift on the body. Life jackets should fit snugly. Finally, people who are severely spastic may not be able to right themselves if they are face down in the water—even if they are wearing a life jacket. In these cases, a Class One U.S. Coast Guard-approved life jacket is recommended. As always, assess each person to see what problems should be anticipated.

Seizures. Persons who experience seizures, especially of the grand mal type, are at special risk. Not only can they fall unconscious into the water, but they may upset the watercraft and everyone else in it. Also, many who experience seizures tend to breathe in deeply during the first moments of the seizure. Most outdoor program agencies require everyone who experiences periodic seizures or black-outs to wear a Class One life jacket when on or in the water. These jackets are not foolproof, but they help to turn unconscious persons face up in the water. Finally, persons who experience seizures should travel in canoes or boats only with staff members or other experienced persons who are aware of their condition. Staff members must be prepared and capable of responding when a person has a seizure in a canoe, boat, raft, or kayak.

Amputees. Missing limbs pose a different type of buoyancy problem. Life jackets are designed to float people with intact limbs. Removal of one or more limbs may cause a person to float on one side or in other positions. People with unusual body shapes should have their life jackets tested.

Life Jackets and Adaptations

Class Three vests. These are the standard "canoeist" type vests that are fairly comfortable and very popular. They work well in most situations. However, they will not turn an unconscious person face up in the water. If loose fitting, these vests have a tendency to slip up around the head in the water, which can be serious if a person does not have enough arm control to hold the jacket down.

Class Two (horse collar) vests. These are the standard life jackets of years ago. Although somewhat uncomfortable, when they are worn properly they help bring a person face up in the water, and they do not slide about. Again, make sure the size and fit are right for individuals.

Class One vests. Class One life jackets are used primarily by ocean vessels that carry passengers. It has ample flotation on the wearer's chest and does the best job of turning an unconscious person face up in the water. *However, Class One vests are not foolproof.* Never rely on it (or any other piece of equipment) to function in every circumstance. Persons who require the use of a Class One vest should ride in a staff member's watercraft or with an experienced person who is a strong swimmer. Class One vests must be properly fitted and worn to be effective. Class One vests may be filled with Kaypok (a Mae West) or may resemble a horse collar. Mae West vests are easily damaged. Always check to make sure the Kaypok bags have not been punctured. The Class One horse collar vest has more flotation; it is made of insulite, and therefore is more rugged. Always check the rating tag on a vest to make certain it is the proper classification.

Class Five vests. These vests are used primarily for whitewater rafting. Actually, a Class Five vest is a cross between a Class Two and a Class Three vest. It provides a little better frontal buoyancy than a Class Three vest and some head support. Class Five vests are recommended for people who have questionable floating characteristics (e.g., people with head injuries or cerebral palsy) but who do not require a Class One vest.

Circulation

Complications caused by poor circulation are less apparent than are other functional disabilities. These complications sometimes involve a lack of sensation, poor coordination of the affected limb, reduced or increased pain, and diminished capability for the body to heal cuts and wounds. Poor circulation may cause the skin to be damaged more quickly when it is wet. Disabling conditions most often affected by poor circulation include diabetes, spinal cord injuries, strokes, head trauma, and multiple sclerosis.

There are few pieces of adapted equipment to combat poor circulation. Some people wear special socks or garments to prevent swelling and to increase blood flow to affected areas. If a person typically uses such devices, they should be encouraged to bring them on an outdoor education or wilderness adventure. The most important safety issues for poor circulation are:

1. If you suspect that a person has poor circulation, ask. This information may be available on the application form. Nevertheless, it should be augmented by personal communication.

2. During outdoor activities where circulation could be a problem (sitting in a canoe), check the affected limbs, especially if there is a loss of sensation. Check for abrasions, blisters, and sores daily. If a sore is discovered, determine whether it is a pressure sore (decubitus ulcer) or simply an abrasion, blister, or cut. Protect it from further injury by bandaging (if open) and eliminating the activity that caused the sore. If you suspect it is a pressure sore, treat it accordingly (see next section on sensation).

3. All skin is susceptible to breakdown when soaked with water or urine. It is important, therefore, to keep it dry, especially for persons who are severely affected by diabetes (brittle diabetics). On a water-based activity such as canoeing, the primary problem is keeping feet dry. Knee high rubber boots work best.

4.   Protect from injury. Due to the slow rate of healing, take extra precautions to protect skin from injuries. The participant should always wear shoes, and when traveling through vegetation, long pants.

Sensation

Two types of sensation are considered here—tactile and visual. A lack of sensation is associated with spinal cord injuries, multiple sclerosis, diabetes, head injuries, and strokes. Although the ramifications of lacking sensation are not always obvious, the consequences of ignoring them outdoors can be severe. Most individuals who are unable to sense pain also experience reduced circulation to the affected limb. This further endangers the limb by retarding healing.

Tactile Impairment

Inability to sense cold and heat. Persons who lack sensation in their extremities will be less likely to know if their feet are cold or hot. If someone appears to be sitting too close to the fire, place a hand on the foot or other area to determine if it is too hot. If in doubt, the person should pull back from the fire. In sub-freezing temperatures, protect against frostbite by insulating the limb well and periodically checking it.

Inability to sense general injury. The infliction of bruises, burns, abrasions, cuts, etc., may not be noticed in a timely fashion by persons who are unable to sense pain. Check immediately if there is reason to believe an injury has occurred. The consequences can be severe if the person is unaware of the injury or continues to engage in an activity that exacerbates the injury.

Pressure sores. Decubitus ulcers are one of the most serious concerns of any person who has a significant lack of sensation. They are caused by continuing pressure on the skin, usually where the skin stretches over a bony prominence in the skeleton, such as the ankles, knees, or the ishial tuberosites in the buttocks. When muscle or skin is pressed between bone and a hard exterior surface, all the blood is squeezed out of the area, which causes tissue death due to a lack of oxygen to the cells.

Tissue death from a pressure sore usually occurs from the inside out. Consequently, it may take a day or two for a pressure sore to become visible. The first sign of a pressure sore is a redness in the skin that does not disappear after the pressure has been removed, or blackened skin. Sometimes it is a hard lump under the skin with little or no visible redness. Unfortunately, these signs, in most cases, suggest that the damage is already done. At the first indication of a pressure sore, all pressure must be removed from the affected area.

The second stage of a pressure sore usually involves a blister in the center of the red spot. The blister eventually ruptures, and the danger of infection increases. In the final stages, the decayed tissue sloughs off, leaving a deep, open wound, possibly to the bone. Throughout this process, which may take a few days or two weeks, the affected person does not feel any pain. The risk of serious infection is great; the wound may take months to heal. In some cases, it may be necessary to amputate the limb. Obviously, the best policy is to prevent pressure sores using the following techniques:

WEIGHT SHIFTS. Many people who sit in wheelchairs shift their bodies every ten minutes or so to allow blood to circulate in the areas under pressure. Referred to as weight shifts, this important daily routine should never be neglected. Weight shifts must be conducted whether the person is sitting in a canoe, raft, or kayak. Staff members should observe, and if necessary, remind people to conduct frequent weight shifts.

SPECIAL PADDING. Spread the weight over as large an area of skin as possible. Bring along plenty of insulite and/or other foam pads to cut and use wherever prolonged pressure against the skin may occur. Often overlooked areas include knees rubbing against the gunwales of a canoe, backbones rubbing against backrests (never assume that a life jacket provides protection against a pressure sore), hips rubbing against the seats and sides of kayaks, and ankles rubbing against the floor or sides of a watercraft. Good sleeping pads are a must; Therma Rest inflatable foam core air mattresses are among the best. These rugged mattresses come in three different thicknesses, but the standard size or the extra thick (Camp Rest) are preferable. Most individuals who use wheelchairs use a seat cushion that should be brought along on an outdoor trip.

Special paddings include:

— Foam cushions, which are made of a dense foam covered by a durable nylon case. They should be kept dry.

— Gel pads, which are heavy, dense, gel wrapped in a tough vinyl case. Gel pads work well and fit nicely on watercraft seats, keeping the center of gravity low. However, they may weigh up to 40 pounds, a burden on portage trails.

— Roho cushions, which are rubber pads consisting of rows of balloons or "teats." These balloons allow more movement on a pressure area and reduce the chances of sores. Also, if a sore occurs, the balloons under the sore can be tied off so that no pressure is placed on the affected area. Roho cushions are bulky, expensive, and can be punctured and rendered useless.

— Jay cushions, which are a combination of solid foam and gel. These cushions are relatively new, but preliminary reports are quite favorable.

DAILY CHECKS. An individual who is susceptible to pressure sores should take along a mirror to inspect difficult-to-view portions of her/his body. Someone else may be willing to check for sores and redness.

Visual Impairments

Visual impairments range from nearsightedness and color blindness to the complete inability to sense light. The necessary adaptations depend on conditions. As always, needed assistance should be discussed with the person.

Night blindness. Some people lack the ability to see at night, which can be serious if a night activity is planned or a person on a camping trip needs to use the latrine after sunset. Usual adaptations include a strong flashlight or a guide with good night vision.

Partial blindness. Some people can sense light or dark, motion, or even distinguish between people and objects. These people may be considered "legally blind" even though they appear to see very well. Often, they use canes to distinguish steps, bumps, rocks, *etc.* If a person who is partially sighted appears to need significant verbal assistance to get around, staff members can ask another participant (perhaps one who is less mobile) to provide help. Accompaniment may be necessary on portages or trails.

Total blindness. A person who is totally blind relies on tactile and audio cues. It may be necessary for a sighted person to provide verbal or physical assistance to help such a person get around in unfamiliar areas.

Special considerations include:

Activity site order. Keep established trails and walkways clear of clutter, such as firewood or equipment. The more the activity sites can be maintained in standard order, the easier it is for people with visual impairments to learn their way around. Some people who are blind may need additional assistance to keep equipment and personal items in order.

Teaching techniques. When teaching lessons on topics requiring physical activity (*e.g.*, taking a water sample or paddling a canoe), provide tactile demonstrations, going through the physical motions with each person who has a significant visual impairment. For less tangible lessons, such as astronomy or ecology, detailed verbal descriptions must be given. Instead of pointing and saying "see that," staff members must verbally describe objects and things. A running dialogue on the terrain, wildlife signs, or a sunset is appreciated by many people with limited vision.

Canes. Most people are familiar with the white canes used by people who are blind. Proficiency with a cane varies with the individual. The white cane is vital equipment and should be so treated.

Guide dogs. Seeing-eye dogs are used by some people to help them get around in the city. If well trained, they may also be a big help in the outdoors. Make certain that the dog remains under control for prolonged periods. In many cases, dogs are trained to respond in a certain way to groups and to attention from others. At the beginning of the program, always have the person who is blind explain to the entire group the way they prefer to have the dog treated.

Motor Control

Many disabling conditions reduce motor control—some permanently and others under certain conditions. To ensure safety in such outdoor tasks as sawing wood, staff members should note the general movement control of a participant with disabilities. The most significant factors to look for are spasticity, tremors, coordination, and hypotonicity (floppy limbs).

Spasticity. Uncontrolled muscle movements are common among people who have cerebral palsy, spinal cord injuries, and multiple sclerosis. Spasticity is characterized by stiffness and resistance to movement in the affected body parts; it also may affect breathing, speech, chewing, and swallowing.

Physical conditions may increase spasticity—cold, fatigue, emotional excitement, or a sudden change of position during a transfer. Spastic muscles sometimes are extremely tight and unmovable; they should never be forced into place or injury may result. In most cases, one can do little but provide a comfortable, supported position and gently allow the spasm to subside.

Most people who have occasional spasticity know its causes and how to cope with it. Ask the affected person. Generally,

— Immersion in cold water will trigger spastic muscles to contract. It may be a safety issue in a program where sudden immersions are possible (*e.g.*, canoe trips).

— Sitting for long periods in canoes and kayaks can cause muscles to spasm.

— Sudden straightening of the legs can cause spasms. Be careful of spasticity when transferring affected persons into a van or canoe.

— Sometimes putting on a life jacket or clothing can be a problem for a person with upper body spasticity. Start with the affected limb first. Ask the participant if there is a preferred method.

Tremors. They are of two types—intention and resting. Both are characterized by uncontrolled shaking. Intention tremors occur with intentional movement, such as picking up a cup or trying to cut food with a knife. Resting tremors occur during inactive periods. Adaptations for tremors are generally the same as for lack of coordination.

Coordination. Many disabling conditions affect general coordination. Gross coordination problems are discussed in the section on balance. A lack of fine motor coordination can be extremely frustrating, not only for the affected person, but also for the onlooker. The more precise the job, the more difficult it will be. Most people affected by this condition compensate the best they can, but to make fine motor tasks easier:

— Provide a stable surface. For example, in outdoor cooking, cut vegetables on a transfer board or paddle rather than over the boiling kettle.

— Use weighted tools, which are easier to control. For example, a canoeist may actually find a heavy paddle easier to use than a lightweight "high-tech" paddle.

— Carry out fine motor activities from a seated rather than a standing position.

Common sense is important. Persons with poor coordination should be supervised and possibly assisted when crossing rough terrain; carrying heavy objects; using saws, knives, or other potentially dangerous items; getting in and out of tents, vans, cars, or boats; and moving or sitting close to fires.

Hypotonicity. This condition is characterized by "floppy" muscles and is typically found among people with muscular dystrophy, post-stroke, and sometimes cerebral palsy. Usually the person has a floppy arm or leg. Sensation also may be affected. Due to lack of muscle tone, a person's joints may be unstable and susceptible to injury. This is important to remember when assisting the person in dressing or transferring. Never pull on the affected limb or the participant's armpit during a transfer—a dislocated joint may result. See Appendix F for a special note concerning the participation in high adventure by persons with mobility impairments.

Seizures. Persons with epilepsy or head injuries are most likely to experience seizures. Seizures vary in intensity, from petit mal to grand mal. Petit mal seizures usually involve a momentary lapse in attention and ability to focus on an activity. Grand mal seizures involve a loss of control, unconsciousness, and uncontrolled muscle spasms. A person experiencing a grand mal seizure may capsize a canoe or kayak or suffer injuries by banging a limb (or head) repeatedly.

MEDICATIONS. Persons who have seizures are almost always on medication, such as dilantin and tegretol. They must maintain strict adherence to their dosage schedule. Be sure to observe the person more closely.

FATIGUE. Persons who experience seizures may be more susceptible when they are fatigued. Staff members should be aware of fatigue levels and make certain that everyone gets enough rest.

AURAS. Many people know in advance when a seizure is imminent. Auras usually precede a seizure by a few seconds but they are not a foolproof warning.

PRECAUTIONS. Seizure activity is not particularly dangerous to an individual's health (unless they are repeated or prolonged). The greatest danger is the lapse in consciousness, especially around water, when operating equipment or machines, or in other situations (around fires) where uninterrupted consciousness is required.

Except for following the prescribed medication schedule and allowing for plenty of rest, there is little that can be done to prevent seizures. Most "adaptations" are simply precautions in the event of a seizure.

1. *Protection from drowning.* Agencies may have policies requiring persons who have experienced seizures within two years of the trip date to:

   — wear a Class One life jacket (see section on buoyancy).

   — travel in a staff member's watercraft or with a highly skilled participant who is aware of and accepts the responsibility for a possible seizure.

   — wear head protection in certain terrain and conditions.

2. *Protection from a fall and awareness by other participants.* Persons who have seizures should disclose this information to the group. If prepared for the eventuality of a seizure, group members can help prevent injury and alleviate possible embarrassment. Many people who have experienced previous head trauma are more vulnerable to severe injury by hitting their heads again. An added danger is the general inaccessibility to professional medical help. Cerebral hemorrhaging while deep in a remote outdoor environment could result in death.

Staff members should be sensitive to the possibility of stigmatizing a participant by requiring that s/he wear special equipment. Many people are self-conscious because they have seizures. Good pre-trip information, a thorough explanation of why they are being asked (required) to wear special equipment, and a reaffirmation that the group accepts and respects them will help the individual to accept the equipment. Although seizures are often associated with some other cognitive impairment, it is incorrect to assume that the individual also has an intellectual deficit. Persons with seizures should be treated like everyone else—rationally and compassionately. Staff members establish this attitude by example.

If or when an individual has a seizure:

1. Protect head and limbs from injury by repeated banging. Cradle the head gently.

2. Encourage other participants to carry on with their normal activities; staring or otherwise drawing undue attention to the person having the seizure may be embarrassing.

3. Never insert anything in the mouth or otherwise try to arrest movement.

Some people experience seizures on a regular basis and prefer to downplay them; seizures are simply a part of their life. Many people also downplay the potential negative consequences of their seizure activity.

Fatigue

Fatigue is a limitation shared by all people. However, certain disabilities affect energy levels and cause fatigue faster than would otherwise be expected. Disabilities that affect fatigue include multiple sclerosis, muscular dystrophy, neurofibromytosis, Friedreich's ataxia, and rheumatoid arthritis. Some medications also may cause fatigue. Seizure activity may induce prolonged fatigue.

External factors affect the rate of fatigue. Persons who have multiple sclerosis may tire faster when it is warm or hot. Persons who have arthritis may experience greater fatigue (and pain) in cold weather. For safety and comfort reasons, staff members must be aware of the fatigue levels of each participant and of the group as a whole. Ask frequently, and remember that some people may be reluctant to admit that they are tired. Good observational skills are extremely important.

Head injuries. Some people with head injuries become fatigued more easily. It is important that they get plenty of sleep. Impaired judgment, paranoia, outbursts, and other behavior problems may result from too little sleep. This situation can be deceptive for the staff and participants, since most people react to a behavior outburst as simply immature, obnoxious, or otherwise unpleasant personality trait. This mistake causes a group to alienate the head-injured participant for behaviors that would not occur if the person had gotten enough sleep. Often a good night's sleep will eliminate undesired behaviors. Staff members must take steps to ensure that other participants who are affected by the disruptive behavior understand the situation and do not hold a grudge against the individual with a head injury.

Multiple sclerosis (M.S.). Persons who have M.S. are more susceptible to fatigue when it is hot or they are overheated. Always make an effort to keep them cool, either by staying in the shade or sponging them off frequently with cool water.

Oftentimes the symptoms of M.S. progress in stages. An individual with M.S. can live for years with no noticeable progression of symptoms. Then the disease may suddenly progress, causing further loss of function. Fatigue can act as a "trigger" for renewed onset.

Another related phenomena is the variance in daily energy levels among people with M.S. One day they can be quite active and energetic, and the next day they can hardly move. Persons with M.S. invariably have less energy than the "average" person. Some people with M.S. in outdoor programs push themselves too hard, only to be unable to get out of bed the following day. Never allow persons with M.S. to work to the point of exhaustion. If in doubt, ask them to refrain from physically demanding activities, like carrying packs over portage trails. Most people know their limits but they need to know that they have the freedom to pace themselves during an activity or refuse an activity altogether.

Seizures. Fatigue may also trigger seizure activity. If a person who experiences seizures has gotten little sleep, or if she has worked particularly hard, expect the frequency of seizures to increase. Except in extraordinary "life-and-death" circumstances, there is no reason to push anyone beyond her physical limits. Just because one person feels good and energetic does not mean that everyone else does. Take it easy and allow plenty of rest opportunities. If other participants question why the group is resting, explain the situation to them.

Diet

Diet limitations affect many people, regardless of a disability. Application forms should specifically request information on dietary restrictions. Diet limitations should be discussed with the participant prior to planning and purchasing food. Each person usually knows the extent of her or his diet limitation and the most appropriate or convenient means of addressing it. Dietary limitations are generally due to one of four conditions:

Medical (e.g., high blood pressure or ulcers). Staff members (and cooks) must be aware of medical diet restrictions. Participants must be asked about diets and food allergies since each individual has idiosyncratic food sensitivities. In many cases, these limitations can be easily avoided by slight adjustments in menus. People on a low-salt diet either use a salt substitute or take food from the kettle before the cook adds salt. In planning menus, staff members should avoid salty foods (such as miso, salted nuts, *etc.*) and/or bring low-salt foods as substitutes. Persons who suffer from ulcers often avoid spicy foods. Therefore, hold off on the hot pepper until after people who have ulcers have received their share of the stir-fried rice.

Allergies. Food allergies also must be known to menu planners. Many individuals are allergic to milk products, some are allergic to wheat, and others may be allergic to almost anything. Avoidance of the food and a supply of substitutes are the only remedies.

Diabetes. Diet limitations due to diabetes are more involved than simply avoiding certain foods. Changing levels of activity alter insulin requirements. The more activity, the less insulin is required. Too much insulin results in insulin shock. Meal times, types of food, availability of snacks, and level of physical activity should be discussed on a daily basis with a person who has diabetes. Once you agree on a schedule for meals, follow it closely. Often a person with diabetes will adjust her or his insulin intake according to anticipated meal times and activity levels. If meal times are delayed, be sure snack food is readily available.

Gastrointestinal (bowel program). Some persons with spinal cord injuries, cerebral palsy, and other disabilities must use suppositories, stool softeners, or digital stimulation to defecate. Usually these people ingest certain medications or foods several hours prior to a planned bowel movement. One of the more common stool softeners is *Colace.* When planning menus, include some natural laxatives, such as bran flakes, prunes, and prune juice.

Judgment

Impaired judgment is the most serious functional impairment a person can experience. Lack of judgment can be frustrating, impede development of "normalized" relationships, and in many outdoor situations, be dangerous. Judgment is not the same as cognition or intelligence. Judgment is defined as the capacity to make rational, reasonable decisions. Many people who are considered cognitively disabled are capable of making reasonable decisions. On the other hand, some highly intelligent persons regularly make poor decisions. Appearances and physical capabilities alone are not good indicators of judgment capabilities.

Persons who are more likely to experience impaired judgment include those with head injuries, strokes, mental retardation (not all, however), and epilepsy. It also can be compounded by memory loss, emotional instability, or loss of self-esteem. Certain medications may also disrupt judgment and decision-making processes. In outdoor programs, coping with participants who have poor judgment can be difficult. Disagreeing with them can be interpreted as an insult or a form of rejection. Despite these obstacles, there are techniques that staff members can use to ensure and facilitate program goals.

Optional Actions to Minimize Effects of Poor Judgment

No immediate action. In many cases, especially when no safety or quality issues are at stake, staff members need not take any immediate action. However, staff members should note examples of poor judgment for later reference.

Indirect intervention. Some displays of poor judgment and decision-making ability are best moderated by indirect influence. A staff member may express her or his opinion in a non-authoritarian manner, or the staff may orchestrate an event to avoid problems arising from poor judgment.

If two persons with poor judgment capabilities go to set up a tent and the staff does not trust their abilities, a staff member can intervene by asking if another participant or staff member can join them. Or, if a person with poor judgment repeatedly offers bad advice to a person who may be easily influenced, the staff can make a discrete effort to keep the two individuals separated. In many instances, indirect intervention may be most appropriate. Staff members should work as a team to coordinate any interventions.

Direct intervention. Occasionally, a staff member must step forward and take control of a situation, especially if safety is an issue or if someone's poor judgment is causing significant disruption or alienation. The staff must take a protective posture to ensure the safety and well being of the group. A participant with poor judgment may insist that she be allowed to paddle a canoe through a section of rough water. If allowing the person to do so significantly increases the probability of capsizing, the staff member should firmly refuse and generally offer an explanation.

Memory Loss

Depending on the nature and type of the impairment, memory loss may present major functional limitations. Although long-term memory loss may be a disruptive life condition, short-term and serial memory loss is of greatest significance to staff members. Participating in an outdoor education or adventure program for a novice requires learning many new techniques, most of which require some degree of short-term memory.

Although degree of memory loss may vary dramatically from person to person, conditions often associated with memory impairment include strokes, cognitive disabilities (*e.g.*, mental retardation), head injuries, spina-bifida (occasionally), mental illness, and certain medications.

Persons with these conditions do not always have noticeable memory impairments. Staff members should engage them in conversations early, asking specific, concrete questions about their lives, interests, and ideas before drawing conclusions about memory quality. Several steps can be followed to minimize the negative effects of short-term memory impairments:

Adjust expectations. Do not expect persons with memory impairments to remember names, details, etc. This caution is critical; staff and other participants may need to remind a person of even the simplest chores on a daily basis. Unless others are familiar with the condition, this situation may be very frustrating.

Explain tasks in simple, progressive steps. Some people may be able only to remember one or two steps at a time. Do not give more information than a person can absorb at any one time. If in doubt about a person's memory, concentrate on conveying only the essential lessons, such as wearing life jackets, no smoking in tents, etc. Sometimes mnemonic rhymes and simple songs can be more easily remembered than straightforward instructions.

Remain vigilant, particularly in regard to safety or getting lost. Accompany persons with significant memory losses on portages and latrine hikes. Be sure to mark tails well.

Do not embarrass a participant in front of others over a memory issue. Many people are self-conscious about memory loss. Be sensitive to their need for acceptance as peers by the group.

Carefully assign activity partners. In assigning activity partners, keep in mind that a person with a memory loss may cause additional frustration for her or his partner. In many cases, a staff members should work with the memory-impaired participant on important activities, such a packing or reviewing the steps to escape an overturned kayak.

Label personal items. Before a camping trip, suggest that participants label personal items. Bring along a marking pen to label socks, underwear, cameras, and other items. This can also be done on short programs where participants bring hats or raincoats. On longer trips, people's patience may wear thin, and overt frustration over someone's inability to find personal equipment, etc., is more likely to erupt. Remember that memory loss, although not readily apparent, may be a serious and permanent condition. Patience from both the staff and other participants is required.

Communication/Language

In any human endeavor, communication between people is vital; clear, thorough communication must be given high priority by the staff. Conscious attention to the communication process is even more important when a participant's ability to communicate is affected by her or his disability.

Hearing Impairment

Programs that integrate people who are hearing impaired or deaf with hearing participants must include an adequate number of sign-language interpreters, but it is not necessary for everyone to know how to sign. Many people who are hearing impaired or deaf are eager to teach the basics of sign language when a person is willing to learn. Staff members can take advantage of this willingness by arranging activities in which learning some sign language is incorporated into the outdoor program.

1.	Staff members should encourage participants to make an effort to learn the ASL (American Sign Language) alphabet and some common signs. Do not be afraid to make mistakes.

2. Bring a pencil and note pad to use when an interpreter is not handy.

3. Some people who are hearing impaired or deaf read lips. When speaking to them, look directly at the person and enunciate words clearly. Exaggerated words are difficult to understand.

Speech Impairment

Persons who slur their words, stutter, or use communication boards are at a disadvantage when trying to communicate. Speech impairments can be very difficult, and at times, frustrating. When integrating people with speech difficulties into a group, staff members must establish a pattern for the group to follow. Never pretend to understand what a person is saying if the message is unclear. Always ask the person to repeat herself until the message is understood.

This process may be cumbersome, but it is honest. To falsely indicate that a message has been understood is an insult. Unfortunately, some people with speech difficulties are so used to being misunderstood that they hesitate to speak at all. Staff members must always take the time to listen and to answer. Too often, other participants grow frustrated and stop making an effort to talk with someone who has a speech difficulty.

Useful techniques in facilitating communication include:

1. When appropriate, phrase questions in a yes or no form. If the affected person has difficulty speaking, ask her/him to blink once for yes and twice for no; or devise some easier means of communicating (e.g., tap once for yes, twice for no).

2. Speech difficulties are increased for some people when they are excited, laughing, cold, etc. If the person is in such a state try to get her or him to relax, warm up, etc.

3. Most people with speech difficulties are easier to understand when their speech patterns become familiar. Patience and careful listening are essential.

Communication/talk boards. Some people with serious speech impairments use communication boards. These boards display the alphabet, common phrases, and perhaps 30-50 commonly used words arranged in a convenient manner. The user communicates by pointing to the word or phrase or by spelling out more complex words. Communication boards work well, but they are slow—especially if a person has difficulty maneuvering her or his hands in place.

Symbol boards. Some people who are unable to read use a board with symbols. For example, Bliss symbols are simplified picture drawings with specific words under each drawing.

Techniques to Use on the Trail

Transferring

The importance of lifting appropriately cannot be overemphasized. Many outdoor leaders suffer back problems later in life from careless lifting during outdoor activities. Knowledge of appropriate body mechanics and lifting techniques when tranferring an individual is critical to avoid back and other injuries. The general principles of lifting are:

1.   Always ask the person being transferred if she would like assistance and how to provide it.

2.   Plan the lift from beginning to end before starting the lift. Carries should know their intended path and final destination.

3.   Lift with your legs, not your back (Figure 5.7). Keep your back erect.

Figure 5.7. Appropriate lifting techniques.

4. If two or more people are performing the transfer, their moves must be coordinated.

5. Turn with your feet, not by rotating your back.

6. Stabilize the surface from which and to which you are transferring. Have other people hold the canoe, wheelchair, etc.

7. Know your strength and fatigue level. Always assess the situation and get the necessary help before you start the lift.

8. Use careful holds. Do not grab armpits, pull on limbs, etc. Special caution is advised for people who have arthritis or other joint conditions.

9. Be careful with catheters and other devices that can be pulled out or damaged during a transfer. Always ask the person being transferred what needs care and special attention.

Types of Transfers

Standing pivot. These transfers work well with people who can bear weight on their legs (Figure 5.8).

Grasp body firmly, but not under armpits. Don't pull on joints.

Stand the participant up, then pivot him/her to new location (canoe, toilet, *etc*).

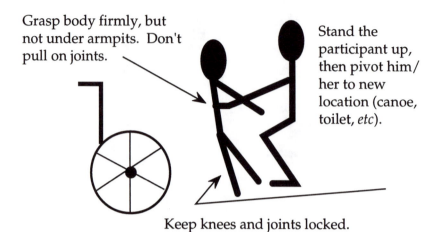

Keep knees and joints locked.

Figure 5.8. Standing pivot.

1. Get as close as possible to the end point of the transfer.

2. Have a secure "hug-type" hold.

3. Count and stand.

4. Pivot to new surface.

5. Gently resume sitting.

Sliding. These transfers work well for people who have good trunk and upper body control and who are transferring between two adjacent and equal height surfaces (wheelchair to toilet, etc.). Place a smooth board from one surface to the other, and help the person slide across, usually under her or his own power. Levels of assistance may vary from holding the board to helping the person balance and slide. (NOTE: Make certain the board is strong and splinter free.)

Two person (top and bottom). This system works well for transferring short distances and if the two lifters are different in height and/or strength. All moves should be planned together.

1. Top lifter (usually the stronger, larger lifter):

— Assist transferee into sitting position.

— Squat behind, reach under the person's arms, and grasp the forearm. It may be better to cross the forearms.

— Support the participant's head with your chest.

— Count and stand.

2. Bottom lifter (usually the shorter, weaker lifter):

— Assist transferee to sitting position.

— Grasp your own forearms underneath the participant's thighs, just above the knees.

— Count and stand.

Two person (side-by-side). This transfer method is good for longer distances and when two lifters are more equal in height and strength; this is also referred to as the fireman's carry.

1. Both lifters squat on either side of participant.

2. Assist participant to sitting position.

3. Lifters lock arms around shoulders of participant.

4. Lifters grasp each other's forearms under participant at mid-thigh.

5. Count and stand. Sometimes it is better to rise to one knee and then to stand up.

Three person. If the participant is too heavy for two people to lift safely, a third person should be employed.

1.   Top lifters:

—   Similar to two person side-by-side: squat on either side of participant.

—   Assist person to sitting position.

—   Participant puts arms around shoulders of lifters.
—   Lifters grasp forearms under participant's legs as far up as possible.

2.   Bottom lifter:

—   Squat in front of participant.

—   Grasp own forearms under legs, just above the knees.

—   Count and stand.

Adaptations to Outdoor Settings

Although the mechanics of lifting work the same in the outdoors as in a hospital, the environmental surfaces are different.

Use spotters. When transferring on difficult terrain, have one or two assistants nearby in case you fall, lose your grasp, or are at risk of dropping the participant.

Stabilize the watercraft. When transferring in or out of a watercraft, be sure to have one or two other people hold the watercraft stable. This can be difficult in waves.

Walk into the water. Bending over to get a person in or out of a watercraft can be difficult on the lifters' backs (especially if they are tall). It is also more dangerous to the participant because of the possibility of being dropped on rocks. Lifters should walk into the water up to mid-thigh, then place the participant into the watercraft without bending over.

Portage Carries and Assists

Some participants must be carried over portage trails. Some agencies may have participants carried by staff members only, or by strong participants who have been trained to transfer and carry. Staff members should never be in a position of relying on other participants to carry someone across a trail. The common types of carries are:

Side-by-side. This carry is appropriate for moderate distances on rough terrain. It also works well when a person is too heavy for one lifter. Simply conduct a two (or three) person side-by-side transfer, then continue down the trail once the participant is up.

Piggy back. Works best for lighter participants or stronger carriers. Most people are familiar with this carry; the most difficult part is getting the participant on and off the lifter. The participant may be able to crawl on the lifter's back while the lifter crouches. The lifter also may sit on the edge of a person's wheelchair, or simply rely on others to help get a participant on the carrier's back.

People pack. This adaptation was designed by Wilderness Inquiry and Gillette Childrens' Hospital in Minnesota. It consists of a pair of shorts (worn by the participant) and a backpack frame (worn by the lifter). The shorts have straps that connect to the frame. This system provides more support for both the lifter and the participant. It also frees up the hands of the lifter. However, it is awkward to get on and off. Also, the shorts should not constrict a person's catheter or abrade the skin.

Assisting people who use wheelchairs over rough terrain. Some people who use wheelchairs are able to navigate trails independently, but most require some assistance, especially over the rough spots.

• Always tip the wheelchair back on its rear wheels. The small front wheels dig in too easily. The person in the wheelchair should be warned before the chair is tipped. Be careful not to grab removable wheelchair parts (*i.e.*, arm rests or foot rests) when lifting or pushing; they may come off and cause injury.

• Have the chair user face uphill. Whether you are going down or up a hill, have the person in the chair facing uphill so she does not fall forward.

• Use seat belts. If the chair is equipped with seat belts, use them during portages.

• On rough terrain it may be easier to have one person pushing in back and one or two pulling up front. Remember to keep the wheelchair tipped so only the back wheels touch the ground.

Wilderness Inquiry Adaptive Equipment

Most people can participate in outdoor education and adventure activities with few special physical adaptations. Wilderness Inquiry relies on group creativity, resourcefulness, and individual desire to ensure that all individuals participate to the fullest extent possible. The agency's adaptive equipment is designed specifically for its program and may not be commercially available (Table 5.1). Contact Wilderness Inquiry (see Appendix D) for more information.

Table 5.1. Wilderness Inquiry adaptive equipment.

Adaptive Equipment	Purpose
1. Sling seat (available from Wilderness Inquiry)	Designed for people with poor balance and trunk control who are unable to sit on a regular canoe seat. It provides lateral and back support. It is similar in concept to a cross between a hammock and a director's chair.
2. *Coleman* seat back (available from *Coleman Company*)	This backrest is attached to a regular canoe seat and provides back support only.
3. One-armed canoe paddle	This paddle attaches to an individual's upper arm so she can paddle with one functional arm.
4. Flexion mitt	This glove is used to secure an individual's hand to a canoe paddle. It is used by people who are unable to grip a paddle.
5. Pulk sled (Available from Wilderness Inquiry)	This cross-country sled was specially designed for people with mobility impairments. A harness system allows it to be pulled by a skier or by dogs.

Tandem bikes offer new opportunities for cycling enthusiasts.

Chapter Six

ACTIVITY PLANS
AND CURRICULUM

Integration strategies work. Mary Jackson teaches fourth grade in an urban school where children with disabilities have recently been integrated. She does not have much background in either science or integration, so she was hesitant about teaching a series of required units on environmental issues. How could she plan a lesson that would excite the children about nature and incorporate those with developmental and physical disabilities into the action?

A major theme for the year at her school is "recycling." Classrooms have been competing to see which one can collect the most aluminum cans and newspapers for recycling. Mary developed the lesson "Recycling Natural Resources" so students could understand that materials we use in our daily activities were created from natural resources (see lesson plan later in this chapter).

The children were divided into cooperative groups with assigned tasks, allowing children with disabilities to participate along with their peers. The "un-nature" hike was held on the paved portion of the playground with teaching and work stations along a marked "trail." Students with mobility impairments could move along the trail with help from others if needed. The activity was a success because the concepts of natural resources and recycling could be illustrated in the seemingly unnatural circumstances of the playground, and because all students could participate. Also, Mary did not need a degree in science to feel comfortable designing and leading this activity.

Outdoor education and high adventure programs are being designed and conducted to include participation opportunities for a range of cognitive and physical abilities. The preceding chapters have described how integrated programs can be planned, managed, and evaluated. This chapter illustrates integration strategies in action. We present six curriculum units that have been used successfully in integrated environments as examples of the possibilities of integrated programming. These units are suitable for use with children and adults, in educational and recreational settings, and by a range of ability levels. The plans are appropriate for school groups, youth recreational groups (e.g., 4-H and Scouts), adults, and adventure outdoor recreation groups.

These curricula are designed according to the outline on the next page.

The first plan, "Nature Activity—Fish Prints," was developed for use in a recreational context. The primary users would be 4-H groups, Scouts, camp or day-camp groups, church youth groups, etc. This is a short, simple, outdoor, education-related group activity that encourages cooperation and includes peers with disabilities. Although the plan presented here is aimed at children, it would be appropriate for adults with some modifications. This activity was field tested by a 4-H group that included children with and without developmental disabilities. The authors appreciate the assistance of Char Schaefer in developing this activity plan.

The second plan, "Nature's Process: Recycling," was developed for school use as part of a ten-session curriculum concentrating on recycling. It is also appropriate for camps, after-school programs, youth groups, outdoor education centers, and community recreation centers. The lesson is designed for fourth-through sixth-grade children. It was field tested at an elementary school by an integrated group that included three children with multiple and severe physical and developmental disabilities. The authors appreciate the assistance of Cheryl Baldwin in developing this activity plan.

The remaining four activity plans are aimed at teaching outdoor recreational skills—cross-country skiing, kayak touring, navigation/map and compass reading, and canoe touring. The lessons can be used with people of all ages and ability levels,

Curriculum/Lesson Plan

Goal. A one- or two-sentence general statement.

Specific objectives. Learner outcomes that are action-oriented, measurable, and tangible.

Intended/appropriate audience. Children/adult; optimal group size; specific disabilities; staff only.

Learning environment.

1. General—required (i.e., ocean, field, river, gym, or park).

2. Specific—optimal learning station within environment (e.g., best place to teach: beach).

Necessary equipment.

Appropriate teaching methods. Lecture, demonstration, movie, slides, reading, or handouts.

Activity.

1. Major content points that must be included.

2. Subtopics in suggested order of presentation.

3. Step-wise progression for teaching each skill.

Follow-up activities.

Evaluation of learner outcomes.

1. Behavior staff should observe if participants absorbed the information presented.

2. Achievable learning outcomes for intended skill levels.

Evaluation of teaching/lesson process.

but they are intended primarily for young adults and adults. The cross-country skiing unit is specific to teaching that skill. The kayak touring and canoe touring units include specific skills (paddling, turning, escaping from an overturned kayak, etc.) as well as covering the range of skills and information needed for safe and efficient participation in an extended kayak or canoe adventure (e.g., packing equipment and landing on beaches to camp). The navigation/map and compass unit can be used on a wilderness trip, in a city park, or on the grounds of a school. All four units were field tested in an outdoor adventure agency program that included participants with a range of physical and cognitive ability levels.

Nature Activity—Fish Prints

Searching for fish in a pond.

Goal. To use natural colors and shapes in a cooperative project—printing an art object.

Specific objectives.

1. Encourage participants to perceive natural and wildlife objects.
2. Develop an understanding and appreciation of colors and shapes that occur in nature and in nature's creatures.
3. Introduce concepts of folk art from other cultures.
4. Encourage children with a range of abilities to cooperatively work and play together.

Intended/appropriate audience. Elementary age children with various abilities, including children with developmental disabilities, in an integrated program.

Learning environment. A variety of environments.

Necessary equipment.

— One fish (a fish with a flat body is best—flounder, halibut, sole, bluegill, or sunfish)
— Water
— Laundry soap
— Paper towels
— Newspapers
— Modeling clay or pieces of styrofoam slightly larger than the fish
— Straight pins
— Nontoxic black or brown acrylic paint, not too thick
— Dish to hold paint
— Materials to hold printing (pieces of soft white or off-white cotton fabric or newsprint; for a more permanent paper print, pliable and absorbent Japanese painting and sketching paper is preferable)
— one-inch paint brushes

Appropriate teaching methods. A very experiential activity. Leader/teacher should give verbal directions and demonstrations at the beginning and then allow the participants to create their own group products.

Activity. Nature printing, using a pigment to transfer an image of a natural object, dates back to humans' early attempts to record objects around them. Many natural printing experiences are possible, including printing with leaves, feathers, weeds, and shells. A specialized art, fish printing originated in the Orient in the early 1800s. It exists today in Japan as "Gyotaku." Completed prints can be shown as works of art, either framed or unframed.

A freshly caught fish or one that has been frozen in a flat position, preferably one with prominent scales, is needed. If using a frozen fish, thaw before using. Select a fish with a flat body to make the printing process easier. Also, beginners will do well to start with a medium-sized fish (6-10 inches long).

This activity can be carried out in conjunction with or as a follow-up to fishing. The use of nontoxic paints permits the fish to be eaten when the printing is completed. Simply wash it off and cook as desired.

In an integrated program, form small groups for the activity. Persons with developmental disabilities should be paired with a peer who can offer guidance if needed. Peers should be instructed in how to assist their teammates.

Instructions to participants (pairs work cooperatively so that everyone contributes and participates):

1. Cover your entire work area with newspaper.

2. Clean the surface of the fish; a clean fish makes a better print. Use soapy water and paper towels to wash the fish several times to remove any debris and mucous. Work gently so you do not damage the fins or remove too many scales.

3. Rinse the fish well and then dry it with paper towels. Blot carefully around the nostrils, in the mouth, and under the gills.

4. Plug up the mouth with small wads of paper to prevent moisture from being squeezed out during the printing process.

5. Discard soiled newspaper after washing the fish and spread out clean newspaper. Place your fish on the table in the position you plan to print.

6. Help each other to roll modelling clay into strips. Place them behind the fins of the fish. (Optional: place your fish on a piece of styrofoam and pin fins to small styrofoam pads.)

7. Spread the fins in a natural position while you pin them to the clay with pins.

8. Working together, apply a thin coat of paint all over the fish. Decide which direction you will paint and brush in that direction only. Each direction gives a different result because the paint is deposited in a different part of the scales. Paint the fins and tail last because the paint will dry there the fastest.

9. Wipe up any excess paint that could spoil the print. Work rather quickly before the paint on the fish dries.

10. Place the cloth or paper to be printed over the painted fish. If using paper, try to avoid wrinkling it.

11. Hold the cloth or paper still while your partner rubs over the entire fish to transfer the paint, first tracing over the mouth, jaw and eye region, then moving toward the tail and the fins, saving the tail for last.

12. Carefully peel the fabric or paper away from the fish to reveal the print.

13. Place the print in a safe place where it can dry thoroughly.

14. The fish must be repainted for each print. A fresh fish usually will make up to ten prints before its exterior becomes clogged with paint.

15. At the end of the activity all members of the group clean up the work areas and wash brushes in soapy water.

Follow-up activities. If this activity has been successful, the leader may move group members to a more advanced stage of printing with other natural materials and the creation of a print collage. For the latter, combine several natural materials (e.g., the materials that exist in the fish environment: weeds, twigs, or flat stones) that can be combined with the fish to create an underwater scene (realistic or imaginary).

Evaluation of learner outcomes. An evaluation can be made by seeing if participants were active in all aspects of the activity, if cooperative interactions took place within groups, if the methods were realistic, and if the participants completed nature prints. Participants can be asked to describe the various parts, colors and shapes of the fish, and the process they went through to create their prints.

Recycling Natural Resources

Cooperative learning to build a bird's nest.

Goals. Natural resources are usable forms of the sun's energy. These valuable, naturally occurring materials include soil, wood, air, water, and minerals. The materials are either renewable, derived from an endless or cyclical source (sun, wind, or water) or nonrenewable, finite in amount (coal, copper, or petroleum). The goals of this activity are to understand that the materials we use in our daily activities were created from natural resources and to facilitate social interactions among all participants.

Specific objectives.

1. To identify whether common products or objects were derived from renewable or nonrenewable resources.

2. To consider ways items can be reused.

Intended/appropriate audience. 12-18 fourth- through sixth-grade children.

Learning environment. See instructional procedures.

Necessary equipment.

— Paper plate
— Record album
— Styrofoam cup
— Aluminum pop can
— Wooden box
— Newspaper
— Worksheet

Appropriate teaching methods. See instructional outline and procedures.

Activity. The students are introduced to the following terms: natural resource, renewable resource, and nonrenewable resource. Students visit pre-established stations. At each station there should be a non-nature object that is commonly used. The students identify the resources used to create that object and decide whether it was created from a renewable or nonrenewable resource. Ways of reusing these materials also are discussed. The activity takes 60-90 minutes.

Instructional Outline

I.   Introduction.

    A. Define natural resource.
    B. Define and give examples of renewable and nonrenewable resources.

II. The un-nature hike.

    A. Set-up.
    B. Stations.

        1. Paper plate.
        2. Record album.
        3. Styrofoam cup.
        4. Aluminum pop can.
        5. Wooden box.
        6. Newspaper.

III. Wrap-up.

    A. Review stations.
    B. Discuss what happens to the items after they have been used.

Instructional Procedures

I.   Introduction.

    A. Provide a workable definition for the term "natural resource." Natural = something that occurs in or is a part of nature, and resource = something that can be used.

    B. A renewable resource is a resource that nature replaces. That is, it has an endless or cyclical source. Examples are

the sun, wind, water, and wood. A nonrenewable resource is a natural resource that is limited in amount.
Because of the scarcity of the resource or the great length
of time it takes to reform once the supply is used, it is
gone.

II. The un-nature hike.

   A. Set-up.

       1. Divide the participants into groups and assign the
          following roles:
          — Recorder, who is responsible for writing down the
            group' s answers.
          — Captain, who is responsible for keeping the group
            together.
          — Investigator, who is responsible for reading the sta-
            tion information.

       2. Each group is given a worksheet (Table 6.1) to fill out
          during its visit to each station. They are to deter-
          mine where the item came from (name the natural
          resource), whether it came from a renewable or
          nonrenewable resource, and to think of another use
          for the item other than that for which it was intended.

   B. Stations. Set up the following stations with appropriate
signs (Table 6.2):

       1. Paper plate (trees, renewable).
       2. Record album (petroleum, nonrenewable).
       3. Styrofoam cup (petroleum, nonrenewable).
       4. Aluminum pop can (aluminum found in earth's
          crust, nonrenewable but recyclable).
       5. Wooden box (trees, renewable).
       6. Newspaper (trees, renewable).

Table 6.1. The un-nature hike worksheet.

Item	Where it came from	Renewable or nonrenewable	Another use for it

Table 6.2. Text for signs at the stations on the un-nature hike.

Station 1	People use me to eat with and then they usually throw me away.
Station 2	You play me to listen to your favorite music.
Station 3	If you go to a fast-food restaurant, they might put your food in me. What am I made of?
Station 4	I hold the soda pop you drink. Most people know I'm recyclable.
Station 5	I'm handy to have around to store things in. I'm sturdy and will be around a long time, but I'm not plastic.
Station 6	People use me to find out what's happening. They read me daily but that's not my only use.

Evaluation of Learner Outcomes:

A. Review the answers for all the stations. Discuss why the participants made their particular choices.

B. Ask the students to explain what generally happens to each of the items at the stations when they have been used as intended.

Cross-country Skiing[*]

Skiing with and without sight.

Goal. To introduce and build on each participant's basic skills in cross-country skiing.

Specific objectives. Given the opportunity, participants will demonstrate knowledge of skis, bindings, boots, and their purposes. In addition, participants will be able to demonstrate or define terms of cross-country skiing (camber, arc, waxes, *etc.*).

Intended/appropriate audience. People of all ages with varying abilities.

Learning environment. Outdoors in winter, three inches of snow.

Necessary equipment. Cross-country skis, boots, poles, and waxes.

Appropriate teaching methods.

---

[*]Reference materials used for this curriculum are:
Jensen, C.R. (1977). *Winter Touring*. Burgess Publishing Co.
O'Hara, R. *Cross-country Skiing*. Minnesota Heritage Series, Minnesota Department of Natural Resources.

— Lecture to be held indoors, one hour in length.
— Demonstration of equipment and methods to be used.
— Lecture on safety awareness, to be held outdoors, 15 minutes in length.
— Opportunity to practice skills.

Activity.

I.   Lecture by cross-country ski instructor.

    A.   The history of cross-country skiing.

    B.   Types of ski equipment.

        1.   Mountaineering ski—wide, strong, with metal edges. Functions best in deep snow and icy, steep terrain. Good when carrying heavy packs, pulling sleds, or telemark skiing.

        2.   General touring ski—wide, lightweight, with medium flexibility. It is ideal for the beginning skier.

        3.   Light touring ski—a fast ski that works well on long tours and requires good balance. It does not work well on ungroomed trails.

        4.   Racing ski—the fastest ski available. It is the narrowest and lightest ski. It requires good balance.

        5.   Poles.

            a.   Types of poles.
               1.   Tonkin (wood-bamboo)—very strong, light, and inexpensive.
               2.   Aluminum or fiberglass—stronger, more durable, and more expensive.

            b.   Straps.
               1.   Straps allow for leverage on the pole and additional thrust in the diagonal stride.
               2.   Look for adjustable straps for proper fit.

  c. Baskets—keep the tips of the poles from sinking too deeply into the snow.

  d. Fitting the poles—poles should measure from the floor to armpit of skier in flat shoes.

6. Boots

  a. Most boots are low cut and lightweight for comfort and ease of movement.

  b. Try on boots with two layers of socks (one light and one heavy).

  c. The four common types of available boots:
   1. High-cut mountain skiing—best for off-track skiing.
   2. General touring—light and durable.
   3. Light touring—light but less durable.
   4. Racing—a light and free-moving boot.

7. Types of bindings.

  a. The cable binding attaches the entire boot to the ski. This type of binding eliminates the need to purchase special cross-country ski boots. It is not often used for general skiing.

  b. The toe binding attaches only the toe of the boot to the ski. This type of binding allows fewer injuries. Many types of toe bindings are available.

8. Waxes.

  a. Types and uses of waxes.
  b. How to apply wax.
  c. It is recommended that waxless skis be used for beginners.

9. Clothing.

    a. Dress in several loose layers of clothing to easily adjust body temperature.
    b. Clothing made of wool or polypropylene is preferable.
    c. Wear two pairs each of gloves and socks, one heavy and one light.
    d. A lightweight hat is needed to prevent loss of body heat.
    e. Regulate body temperature by adding or removing layers of clothing.

II. Cross-country ski demonstration.

    A. Proper methods of putting on the equipment.

    B. Move and balance without the use of ski poles.

    C. Proper posture.

    D. Step and glide with arms swinging in opposite direction of feet.

    E. Proper use and grasping of poles.

    F. Going uphill.

        1. Requires slightly bent knees with a forward lean for a better propelling motion.

        2. Traversing is a wide slow zigzag motion.

        3. Diagonal stride provides quick thrusts and glides at a faster pace.

        4. Herringbone is a fast-paced method and works well on a short steep hill (this is for a strong skier). The tips of the skis are spread apart. The motion is a constant thrust with no glide and a setting motion to the in-side of the ski.

     5. The side step takes small steps (6-12 inches apart) up the hill.

     6. The trot is a quick forward step much like that of the thrust and glide motion, but without the glide.

  G. Going downhill.

     1. Keep knees bent and keep skis parallel and close. Hold the poles close to the body with the tips of the poles pointed behind the body.

     2. Snowplow to control speed.

  H. Falling properly—sit down to one side, tucking poles behind the body. Do not fall on knees because they are prone to injury.

  I. Turns.

  J. Demonstrate skate-skiing methods for those interested.

III. Safety awareness on the tour.

  A. Essentials for a short tour.

     1. Fluids (avoid alcohol).
     2. Food (high in carbohydrates, hard candies, dried meat, dried fruit, granola, hard breads).
     3. Matches and fire starter.
     4. Extra clothing (dry mittens, socks, and hat).
     5. Area map and compass.
     6. Stay within half a day of shelter.
     7. Plan on finishing tour by dark.

  B. Check all equipment before the tour.

Follow-up activities.

1. Follow-up opportunities include ski clubs; local park systems (many have rentals and groomed trails); area lakes

(groomed and ungroomed trails but typically no rentals); state parks (groomed and ungroomed trails); and private rentals (with groomed trails).

2. Written information for participants on how to choose equipment and locations of future participations.

Evaluation of learner outcomes. Participants should be able to demonstrate the ability to:

1. Put on and take off skis.
2. Check boots and bindings for proper fit.
3. Stride and balance without the use of ski poles.
4. Glide with rhythm.
5. Demonstrate the proper use of poles.
6. Go uphill.
7. Go downhill.
8. Fall properly.
9. Understanding safety awareness.

Evaluation of teaching/lesson process. Participants will have the opportunity to complete a written evaluation.

Kayak Touring

Goal. To develop skills that will give participants basic knowledge in all aspects of sea kayaking, including kayak touring.

Specific objectives. These lessons are designed to be used for sea kayaking trips. These lessons are intended to inform participants of:

1. The potential safety hazards in sea kayaking.
2. The precautions required for safe sea kayaking, including use of PFDs and wet suits, traveling in groups, and weather awareness.
3. The techniques for safe, effective sea kayaking including packing, launching and landing, paddling, and wet exits.
4. Proper care of all sea kayaking equipment.

Kayaking together in British Columbia's Queen Charlotte Islands.

Intended/appropriate audience. Participants on a sea kayaking trip. Ideal group size is 10-15 participants.

Learning environment.

1. General—on water; lake, river, ocean, or pool.
2. Specific—dry land instruction area available, and calm water area.

Necessary equipment.

— Kayaks
— Double-bladed paddles, offset or parallel blades
— Life jackets
— Wet or dry suits

Appropriate teaching methods. Lecture, demonstration, handouts, and reference books.

Activity. These lessons are designed to be used within the first two days of any sea kayaking trip.

I. Safety awareness.

   A. Why? Discussion of safety hazards at the beginning of the trip serves:

      1. To reinforce safety awareness within the group.
      2. To provide reassurance to participants who are unfamiliar with sea kayaking.

   B. When? Once the whole group is together and not on the water (at a lunch stop, while driving to the site, after dinner the first night, or by the boats before anyone starts working with the equipment).

   C. Methods. Question-and-answer and discussion.

   D. Lesson.

      1. Introduce the concept of safety. "A priority for this trip is that it's a safe trip. The best insurance is to avoid potential problems while sea kayaking."

      2. Ask participants to name potential problems. "We need to be aware of what may go wrong. We'd like everyone to try to think of something that might happen while sea kayaking that could become a safety problem. It may even be the nightmare that kept you awake last night."

      3. Ask participants to suggest reasonable precautions for each potential problem. Use this time to introduce safety policies. "Think of what we need to do to make sure a problem never happens or how to fix things if it does happen."

      4. Topics should include:

         a. Use of PFDs (personal flotation devices)— always worn just in case you tip over.

b. Use of wet and semi-dry suits—always worn if the water temperature is below 60 degrees.

c. Traveling in groups—this is the best safety precaution for tipping and getting lost.

d. Tipping and wet exits.
    1. Avoid these by packing the kayaks carefully and keeping your weight low.
    2. If it happens, it's OK.
        — We'll teach you wet exits.
        — Help is always close when traveling in groups.
        — We can get the kayak emptied and ready again.
        — Shore will usually not be far away.

e. Hypothermia.
    1. Avoid it by using wet/semi-dry suit and pacing yourself.
    2. If you are cold, say so. Then we can:
        — Get you someplace warmer.
        — Help you to exercise to warm up.
        — Get you food and drinks (maybe hot drinks).
    3. Watch each other for signs of hypothermia (people may not recognize it in themselves).
        — Shivering.
        — Change of color (blue or purple lips and fingers).
        — Confusion.
        — Mood swings.

f. Sea animals—give them room.

g. Big waves/swells.
    1. Can be safely handled in kayaks by turning into them at an angle but it is best to avoid them by watching the weather.

2. If they start to come up, follow staff members.
3. Always pay attention to shore and charts to note potential landing areas, which are wind sheltered and not likely to have large swells.

   h. Currents, tides, and other hazards of moving water—travel in groups so staff members can help everyone to avoid these hazards.

5. Reassure participants that safety precautions will be taken. Remind them that they must assume responsibility for their own safety as well as for the safety of the group, by following the precautions.

6. Encourage participants to think and talk about safety throughout the trip.

E. Evaluation: Staff members should see that participants:

1. Follow safety policies.
2. Remind each other to follow safety policies.
3. Appear to be assured and confident about trip safety; if not, the staff needs to provide additional lessons.

II. Kayaking equipment.

A. Why? Participants should be taught enough about the equipment so they:

1. Have the basic vocabulary needed to easily work together using the kayaks.
2. Know how to properly care for all the equipment.

B. When? This lesson is to be used just before the group is issued kayaking equipment.

C. Methods. Demonstration and lecture—the more often staff members use the appropriate names while using/ pointing to equipment, the easier it will be for participants to learn the terminology.

D. Lesson.

   1.   Introduce by associating equipment and safety. "When we talked about safety and how to keep this trip safe, we mentioned some special equipment we use sea kayaking, such as PFDs and wet/semi-dry suits. All the equipment is important for a safe trip. Because of that, it's important to make sure all the equipment is working well. When we show the equipment and how to use it, we also mention some tips on how to take care of it. We urge participants to follow the tips."

   2.   Introduce the "big 5" (kayak, paddle, spray skirt, wet suit, and PFDs) and their parts:

      a. Kayaks.
         1. Cockpit.
         2. Seat.
         3. Footpegs—how to adjust and use.
         4. Cockpit combing—reinforced to support up to 150 pounds.
         5. Deck—not built to support weight, do not sit on it.
         6. Bow—front of a dog goes bow-wow; front of the kayak is the bow.
         7. Stern.
         8. Hatches.
         9. Waterproof storage only if the seal is good.
            — Keep sand out of the seal.
            — Wash the seal occasionally.
        10. Rudders—remember to pull up when landing.

      b. Paddles.
         1. Blade of the paddle is like the blade of a knife.
         2. Protect the blade of the paddle from sand and rocks.

3. Rest it on your foot or something soft when you hold it upright.
4. Avoid banging paddle on the kayak when paddling.

c. Spray skirt.
   1. Needs to seal tightly around cockpit and your waist.
   2. Protect from sand and rocks.

d. Wet and semi-dry suits.
   1. Who wears which:
      — Everyone may need one for safety reasons.
      — Fragile (and expensive).
   2. Handle with care. "Sand is uncomfortable and bad for the suits— avoid it. Always wear shorts or protective pants outside to help keep from wearing out the seat of the suit. Do not kneel in sand or rocks when wearing the suits."
   3. When to wear depends on:
      — Water temperature.
      — Distance from shore (crossings).
      — Body type/body fat content.
   4. Demonstrate how to put each on. "They are not easy to get in and out of; toilet before entering."

e. PFDs
   1. Explain types
      — Class One—those with seizure disorders must wear a Class One.
      — Class Two
      — Class Three
      — Class Five
   2 Demonstrate sizing and how to put them on.
   3. Always wear them. Avoid sand and abrasion and filth. When you're not wearing them, put them in a safe place.

Never sit on a PFD. Sitting on them causes excessive wear on the material. PFDs make great pillows.

3. Adaptive equipment.

    a. What it is.
        1. Crazy Creek chairs.
        2. Flexion mitts.

    b. How it is used.

4. Safety equipment.

    a. Extra paddle.
    b. Pumps.
    c. Sponges.
    d. Throw rope.
    e. Weather radio.
    f. Repair kit.

5. Wet exits and rescues.

    a. Demonstrate wet exits.
        1. Pull the rip cord.
        2. Put hands on kayak beside your hips.
        3. Push yourself away from the kayak.

    b. Rescues.

    c. Demonstrate use of:
        1. Paddle floats.
            — Improvised.
            — Custom built.
        2. Pumps.
        3. Sponges.

E. Evaluation. Participants should be able to:

    1. Take care of the equipment.

   2. Understand the basic kayaking terminology used by
       staff members.
   3. Perform wet exits.

III. Packing the kayaks.

   A. Why? Participants should learn how to:

       1. Pack equipment so it stays dry.
       2. Pack equipment securely.
       3. Pack kayaks so they are well balanced.
       4. Pack unusual equipment, such as wheelchairs.

   B. When? Immediately before loading the kayaks for the
       first time.

   C. Methods. Demonstration and lecture.

   D. Lesson.

       1. Show where equipment can be stored:

           a. In hatches.
           b. Around seats.
           c. Not in the rudder system.

       2. How to pack in dry bags.

           a. Care of dry bags.
               1. Fragile: Do *not* drag them.
               2. Avoid abrasions and sharp points.

           b. How to pack dry bags—choose what you need to
               keep dry: wool clothes/sleeping bag.

           c. Place what you might need first toward the top.

           d. Avoid sharp objects—they can cut the bags from
               the inside.

    e. Alternatives to dry bags.

    f. Double line sleeping bag, stuff sack with plastic bags—squeeze the air out.
        1. If all the air is out, it is small, but rock hard.
        2. If most of the air is out, it is fairly small and still flexible so it can fill spaces.
        3. Demonstrate proper seal.

3. Plan a packing strategy.

    a. Avoid getting sand and debris in the kayak.
    b. Put all that needs to go into the kayak in one place.
    c. This is important to estimate space and weight needs.
    d. Divide into piles for each compartment based on space and weight.

4. Load the kayak.

    a. Kayak should float in still, shallow water.
    b. Load hatches, making sure kayak stays balanced.
    c. Load equipment around seats, packing and lashing so it stays in place.
    d. Put wheelchairs in the middle hatch. Make sure the weight is low and they are covered to avoid salt corrosion.

5. Loading on land.

    a. Essentially, it seldom happens.
    b. If the water is that rough, stay in camp.
    c. If you have to move a full boat into water, carry with lots of people and boat slings.
    d. Demonstrate the use of the boat slings.

6. Try to remember packing strategy.

E. Evaluation. Kayaks should be properly balanced when loaded.

IV. Paddling techniques.

    A. Why? Participants should be taught:

        1. How to hold the paddle.
        2. Basic strokes: forward stroke, sweep, draw, reverse, and brace.

    B. When? Just before the first time participants paddle the kayaks.

    C. Methods. Demonstration and lecture, if possible, on a sandy beach area.

    D. Lesson.

        1. Show how to hold the paddle.

            a. Proper placement of your hands.
                1. Rest paddle, centered, on top of your head.
                2. Reach up and grab the paddle so your elbows make a right angle. This puts hands in the proper position.
                3. Death grips are tiring and unhealthy. Relax your grip on each stroke by opening fingers of top hand.

            b. Proper blade angle.
                1. The right hand is the gripping hand.
                2. The ridge of your knuckles lines up with the side edge of the paddle blade.
                3. This hand often controls the angle of the paddle.
                4. The left hand grips the paddle loosely so the blade angle can change.

            c. Feathered vs. non-feathered blades.
                1. Feathered.
                    — Requires wrist movement. Right wrist flat when one pulls blade through the

water. Right wrist cocks up on paddle recovery. Left hand loosens grip to make this possible.
— Advantages: Stronger pull for some and the blade in the air cuts the wind instead of acting like a sail.
2. Non-feathered. You do not have to coordinate the wrist action while paddling.

2. Basic strokes. Demonstrate these, preferably using a long stick or paddle shaft to make the strokes in the sand; this makes the demonstration more visible to participants.

a. *Forward stroke.* Moves kayak forward.
1. Pulling side.
— Reach hand as far forward as possible.
— Turn torso but do not bend at the waist.
— Bury the blade in the water.
— Pull elbow straight back to your waist while pushing forward with end of paddle not in the water.
2. Recovery side.
— Relax grip of recovery hand on the paddle (prevents fatigue).
— Punch hand forward at shoulder level.
— Hand and elbow never go above your shoulder.
— Hand never crosses the center of the boat.
3. Avoid banging paddle on the kayak deck.
4. The more water you move, the more you'll move forward.
5. Bury the blade in the water.
6. Use as much of your body as you can. Turn torso. Push against footpegs. Keep elbow in line with sides of your body (protects shoulders from dislocations).
7. Pace yourself. Try to find a rhythm like you would for a long bicycle ride.

b. *Sweep*. Turns kayak.
   1. Like forward stroke but blade stays near the surface of the water.
   2. Blade makes a sweep instead of staying near center line of the kayak.
   3. Motion is made by turning torso rather than pulling the elbow back to the waist.

c. *Draw*. Moves kayak sideways.
   1. Reach straight to the side.
   2. This is the only stroke that requires both hands to be on the same side of your body.
   3. The whole paddle stays vertical.
   4. Bury the blade in the water, flat side facing you.
   5. Pull the blade toward you by pulling wrist to your waist and upper wrist toward your nose.
   6. Recovery.
      — Turn shaft of underwater paddle so paddle blade is at a right angle to the kayak.
      — Push paddle away from kayak with the blade cutting the water.
      Repeat draw motion.
      — An alternative way to recover is to lift the blade clear of the water. Reach far to the side of the kayak. Bury the blade in the water. Repeat draw motion.

d. *Reverse*. Moves kayak backwards or at least slows it down.
   1. Stroke side.
      — Turn torso and look backwards over your shoulder.
      — Keep your elbow in line with the plane of your body to protect your shoulders.
      — Bury the paddle blade in the water by straightening your elbow and dropping your hand towards the water.

— Turn your torso to bring your hand and the paddle blade forward.
2. Recovery side.
— Bend elbow to lift fist up towards your shoulder—this lifts the paddle blade up and out of the water.
— Turn torso (while making a reserve stroke on the stroke side).
— Now you are ready to bury the paddle blade behind you.
3. Rudder system. Can confuse steering when going in reverse. Pull up on rudder cord to lift rudder out of the water.

e. *Brace.* Balances/stabilizes the kayak.
1. Turn paddle blade so flat surface parallels the water surface.
2. Push down on the surface of the water with the paddle blade.

E. Evaluation. Participants should:

1. Be able to execute the five basic strokes when verbally instructed to do so.
2. Have some idea of how each stroke will move the kayak.

V. Launching and landing.

A. Why? Participants should know the theory behind landing and launching a kayak:

1. Without flipping.
2. Without damaging the kayak.

B. When? Before launching or landing for the first time.

C. Methods. Lecture and demonstration.

D. Lesson.

1. Where to launch and land.

   a. Picking the right spot is key to making it easier.
      1. Always look for potential landing spots.
      2. Things to look for:
         — Wind-sheltered area.
         — Little or no big waves.
         — Beach.
         — No "kayak-eating" rocks.

   b. Land before you really need to so you can be picky about where to land.

2. Launching techniques while in surf.

   a. Bow paddler gets into the kayak while the bow is floating.

   b. Stern paddler gets into the kayak.

   c. Look for a lull in the waves.
      1. Waves usually come in groups of six or eight.
      2. Usually a lull between wave groups.

   d. Launch during a lull. If possible, place hands in the sand on both sides of the kayak.

   e. One hand must continue to hold the paddle, but you can still use that fist for support.
      1. Support your weight with your hands.
      2. Hitch the kayak forward—preferably with help.

   f. Do this with as little weight as possible on the kayak.

   g. Once the kayak is floating, paddle quickly to clear the breaking surf.

   h. After launching, wait for the group to get into paddling formation.

NOTE: *The most experienced kayakers are the last ones to launch. They help less experienced people get going.*

3. Surf landing techniques.

   a. Surf landings are one of the most dangerous aspects of sea kayaking. Whenever possible avoid them! If you cannot avoid them, wait outside of where the waves are breaking for an opportunity to land.
      1. Land one kayak at a time.
      2. Choose a lull in the waves.
      3. The most experienced kayaker lands first. Second most experienced kayaker lands last and provides instruction to others.

   b. Land.
      1. Paddle in on the *back* of a wave. Riding the front of the wave usually tips the kayak or smashes it into shore.
      2. In most cases, you should be able to keep pace with the wave.
      3. If the wave passes you, reverse stroke until you are on the back of the next wave. Keep perpendicular to waves.
      4. Repeat this process until you actually land.
      5. Get out of the kayak quickly and secure it so it isn't smashed by the surf.

NOTE: *If you are accidentally turned sideways and a wave is about to break over you, brace into the wave. This will help keep you from capsizing.*

E. Evaluation. Participants should understand:

1. How to select good launching and landing sites.
2. How to make a safe landing.

Follow-up activities.

— Local kayak club.
— Local lakes, rivers, and places to kayak.
— Local rental/retail outlets or dealers.
— More advanced learning opportunities.
— Other learning opportunities.

Evaluation of learner outcomes.

1. Review each specific objective to determine if all learners have achieved those objectives.

2. Methods to evaluate include:

    — Observe participants performing activities.
    — Observe safety procedures used by participants.
    — Ask participants questions related to information given in lesson.
    — Ask participants for evaluative feedback.

Evaluation of teaching/lesson process.

1. Written evaluation of teaching process.
2. Verbal evaluation of teaching process.
3. Observation of participants performing the skill.
4. Unsolicited comments from participants, care providers, and staff members.

Navigation/Map and Compass Reading*

Goal. To develop the skill of using a map and compass and successful navigation for a canoe or kayak trip.

---

*Reference material used for this curriculum is:
Kjellstrom, B. (1972). *Be an Expert With Map and Compass.* LaPorte, IN: American Orienteering Service.

Learning to use a topographical map in the wilderness.

Specific objectives.

1. Learn the parts of a compass and its basic use.
2. Learn how to interpret and use a topographic map or chart.
3. Use the map and compass together to find a position and to plan a course.

Intended/appropriate audience. People of all ages and ability levels can participate. Persons can be paired or placed in small groups with complementary abilities. The level of content can be adjusted for the ability levels of participants.

Learning environment. Both indoor and outdoor areas can be used. The best environment is outdoors in an area covered by the map used; in an open area where landmarks (shown on the map) can be seen in the distance; and in an area where participants can comfortably spread out maps and work in teams.

Necessary equipment. One compass and one map for every two persons is ideal. It is possible to conduct the activity using one compass per couple and having one map per group of four. Larger numbers using maps and compasses will result in only a few participants having enough access to maps to understand the process.

The compasses should have a transparent base plate with a direction of travel arrow. Maps should be designed for navigation purposes, and if the lesson is on a trip, the maps should cover the entire area to be traveled. They should include topographics, declination of magnetic north, meridian lines, scale of distance, and contour interval. U.S.G.S., McKenzie, or Canadian Geological Service maps or navigation charts should be used.

Appropriate teaching methods. Lecture, demonstration, and practice opportunities should be given in the first few days if on an adventure trip. A good time for an introductory lesson would be at a lunch stop or at a campsite just before setting out for the day's journey so the information learned can be tied to the reality of moving from one spot to another while "staying found." Match participants into pairs or small groups with complementary abilities for the lesson. Distribute maps and compasses.

Activity. Map and compass use can appear to be very confusing to some participants. Some may view it as "magic" that only the leader really needs to know. Some will avoid dealing with maps, a compass, and the navigation process because they feel intimidated by the process. The leader needs to start off the lesson by making it a non-threatening topic, one that everyone can and should learn. Navigation is a vital ingredient of wilderness travel. It is a skill that can give participants a great amount of freedom and confidence that they can now access the wilderness on their own or with friends. Getting lost in the wilderness is often a beginner's greatest fear about wilderness travel. The leader should stress that the basic goal of wilderness navigation is to avoid getting lost by always "staying found," by constantly checking their position so they know where they are and where they are going.

I. Compass parts.

A. *Base plate* is the clear plastic, rectangular piece on which the compass rests.

B. *Graduated dial* contains the degrees located around the outside of the compass. How many degrees are there, and how many degrees does each line indicate?

C. *Direction of travel arrow* is on the base plate, it may read "Read bearing here."

D. *Magnetic needle* is usually red and moves when the compass is moved. It rotates on a central pivot. It always points to "magnetic north."

E. *Meridian lines* are on the bottom of the compass below the magnetic needle.

F. *Measuring scales* on the edge of the base plate are usually in inches and millimeters.

G. The magnetic needle is susceptible to influence from metal objects like belt buckles, knives, and other compasses. Demonstrate this for participants.

II. *Magnetic north and true north. True north* is the pole at the geographic top of the earth. If looking at a globe, it is the very top of the earth where the globe is attached to its stand. Most maps and charts are oriented according to true north. *Magnetic north* is the pole where the magnetic fields come together. The magnetic fields are caused by minerals and rocks in the earth. The magnetic compass always points toward the magnetic north pole, not the true north pole. The magnetic north pole is located about 600 miles south of the true north pole on a longitude of about Chicago. So, if one is in Chicago, the two poles line up and the magnetic compass pointing toward the magnetic north pole is also pointing at the true north pole. But, as one goes to either side of this Chicago line of longitude, there is a difference between magnetic north and true north. This difference is called "declination." This difference is usually about 3-4 degrees in the Minnesota area, which is a negligible difference. But in other areas it is significant. In Montana, the declination is about 17 degrees, and in the Northwest Territories of Canada it is about 24 degrees. So, the concern about converting magnetic direction to true north varies with your location. We will talk about this more when we look at the maps.

III. Map components.

A. The top of the map (or chart) is always true north; the map is oriented to true north, not magnetic north.

B. Locate the mileage scale. How many inches per mile?

C. Locate topographic lines. Explain that these lines connect equal points of elevation. A contour interval is shown in the index, it is the difference in elevation from one line to another. The closer together the lines, the steeper the incline, the farther apart, the more level the terrain is. Indicate hills, valleys, ridge lines, peaks, flat areas, etc., for participants.

D. Locate meridians running north and south at set intervals. They are used to position the map and compass to true north.

E. Point out map symbols like portages, wooded and open terrain, buildings, streams, lakes, water depths, etc.

IV. Orienting the map to true north.

A. Determine the declination from the map. Set the compass for the declination by picking up the compass, reading the direction of travel arrow, turn the graduated dial to adjust for declination. If the declination is east, subtract the declination from 360 degrees and set the dial on the resulting number. For example, if the declination is 17 degrees east, set the dial on 343 degrees. If the declination is west, add it to 360 degrees and set the dial accordingly.

B. After setting the declination, place the compass on the map with the edge of the base plate lined up with the edge of the map or one of the meridian lines on the map. The direction of travel arrow should point to the top of the map. Now turn the entire map, with the compass lined up with the edge, until the magnetic needle (red needle) lines up with the meridian lines at the bottom of the compass. The map is now oriented to true north.

V. Locating a position.

    A. On the map, indicate your approximate position to the participants. Use the map and the surrounding terrain to help participants locate landmarks. Explain how important and useful it is to have the map oriented every time one wants to locate positions and chart courses.

    B. Explain how to use landmarks like points, bays, peaks, valleys, campsites, and islands to locate a position by using triangulation. It may be too complicated at this point to explain shooting bearings to these landmarks. That can wait for a more advanced lesson.

    C. If on a canoe trip, explain how to find portages by looking for low spots on the ridge line, the portages usually follow the lower areas and drainages.

VI. Following a bearing to a destination.

    A. The compass and map are often used to determine a direction of travel to a destination. Once the direction is determined, the compass can be followed until the destination is reached.

    B. Orient the map to true north. Locate your present position on the map.

    C. Find a destination on the map to which you would want to travel; it may be a hill, a portage, a point, or a campsite.

    D. On the map, line up the "direction of travel" arrow, or the long edge of the compass base, on your current position and pointing to your intended position.

    E. Rotate the graduated dial until the meridian lines on the bottom of the compass line up with the magnetic needle (red needle) of the compass. The degree reading at the "direction of travel" or "read bearing here" arrow or line is the bearing of your intended destination.

Pick up the compass, hold it flat in front of your nose with the "direction of travel" arrow pointing directly away from your nose. Turn your entire body until the red magnetic needle lines up with the meridian lines on the bottom on the compass. Your nose is now pointing directly toward your destination. Pick out a landmark in line with the bearing of the destination and travel to that landmark. Once you reach it, again use the compass to get a sight on the next landmark in line with the compass bearing. Set on the same bearing, hold the compass in front of your nose, and rotate your body, not the compass, to find the bearing of the destination. Once the destination is reached, consult the map again to determine the bearing of the next destination.

Follow-up activities. Encourage participants to practice compass navigation skills throughout the trip or outdoor activity when they are moving, at lunch or rest stops, and in the mornings before setting out for the day. These skills are easy to forget if not practiced.

Teach participants how to "shoot" bearings to landmarks, transfer these lines of position to the map, and find their position by using triangulation.

Conduct a miniature orienteering game as follows: Place a coin on the ground. Set the compass to 0 degrees, walk 50 paces on that bearing. Set the compass to 90 degrees, walk 50 paces on that bearing. Set the compass to 180 degrees, walk 50 paces. Set the compass on 270 degrees, walk 50 paces. That is where the coin should be.

Evaluation of learner outcomes. At the end of the lesson, participants should be able to orient the map to true north, locate primary landmarks on the map, set a compass to a bearing, and use the map and compass to determine a bearing to a destination. The instructor can evaluate the level of understanding by observing the participants during the lesson and by observing the proficiency of map and compass use on the activity or trip after the lesson.

Evaluation of teaching/lesson process. Ask participants how they felt about the lesson; was it clear and understandable, was there enough instruction, was there enough time given to the various lesson components, was there enough practice opportunity? Ask other leaders if the lesson was effective. Observe the results; do participants appear to understand navigation enough so they can do it during the trip?

Canoe Touring

Goal. To develop skills that will give participants basic knowledge in all aspects of canoeing, including canoe touring.

Specific objectives. These lessons are designed to be used on program canoe trips. They provide the basic organization and information needed for participants to canoe safely. These lessons are intended to inform participants of:

1. The potential safety hazards in canoeing and canoe touring.
2. The precautions required for safe canoeing, including use of personal flotation devices (PFDs), traveling in groups, and weather awareness.
3. The techniques for safe, effective canoeing, including packing, launching and landing, paddling, and water rescues.
4. Proper care of all canoeing equipment.

Intended/appropriate audience. Participants on a canoe touring trip. Portions of this lesson (safety awareness, canoe equipment, and paddling techniques) are also appropriate for a one-day canoe experience on a local lake or river. Ideal group size is 10-15 participants.

Learning environment.

1. General—a lake, river, protected bay, or pool.
2. Specific—dry land instruction area available and calm water area.

Necessary equipment.

— Canoes
— Paddles

Canoe touring

— Adapted paddles
— Padding (insulite foam in appropriate sizes)
— Personal flotation devices (PFDs)

Appropriate teaching methods. Lecture, demonstration, handouts, and reference books.
Activity. These lessons are designed to be used as initial instruction if a one-day activity or within the first two days of any canoe touring trip.

I.   Safety awareness.

    A. Why? Encouraging discussion of potential safety hazards at the beginning of the trip serves to:

        1. Reinforce safety awareness within the group.
        2. Provides reassurance to participants who are unfamiliar with canoeing.

    B. When? Once the whole group is together and before the group is ever on the water (at a lunch stop while driving to the site, after dinner the first night, or by the boats before anyone starts working with the equipment).

C. Methods. Question-and-answer and discussion.

D. Lesson.

    1. Introduce the concept of safety. "A priority for this trip is that it is a safe trip. The best insurance is to avoid potential problems while canoeing."

    2. Ask participants to name potential problems. "We need to think about what might go wrong. We would like everyone to try to think of something that might happen while canoeing that could become a safety problem. It may have been the nightmare that kept you awake last night."

    3. Ask participants to suggest reasonable precautions for each potential problem. Use this time to introduce safety policies. "Think of what we'd need to do to make sure a problem never happens or how to fix things if it does happen."

    4. Topics covered.

        a. Use of PFDs—always worn just in case you tip over.

        b. Traveling in groups—this is the best safety precaution for tipping and getting lost.

        c. Tipping. Avoid this by packing the canoes carefully and keeping your weight low. If it happens, it's OK. We will teach you what to do. Help is always close because we will travel in groups. Shore will usually not be far away.

        d. Hypothermia—avoid it by using wool or polypropylene, staying fairly dry and pacing yourselves. If you are cold, say so. Then we can get you someplace warmer, help you to exercise to warm up, and get you food and drinks (maybe hot drinks). Watch each other for signs of hypothermia (people may not recognize it in themselves): shivering, change of color (blue or purple lips and fingers), confusion, mood swings.

e. Bad weather or rough water—avoid them by watching the weather. If they start to appear, follow staff to shore. Always pay attention to the shore and note potential, protected landings (wind sheltered and not likely to have large swells).

f. Rapids and other hazards of moving water— travel in groups so staff members can help everyone to avoid them.

5. Reassure participants that safety precautions will be taken. Remind them that they must assume responsibility for their own safety, as well as the safety of the group, by following the precautions.

6. Encourage participants to think about and talk about safety throughout the trip.

E. Evaluation. Staff members should see that participants:

1. Follow safety policies.
2. Remind each other to follow safety policies.
3. Appear to be more assured and confident about trip safety. If not, the staff members need to provide additional lessons on safety.

II. Canoeing equipment.

A. Why? Participants should be taught enough about the equipment so they:

1. Have the basic vocabulary needed to easily work together using the canoes.
2. Know how to properly care for all the equipment.

B. When? This lesson is to be used just before the group is issued canoeing equipment.

C. Methods. Demonstration and lecture. The more often staff members use the appropriate names while using/pointing to equipment, the easier it will be for participants to learn the terminology.

D. Lesson.

1. Introduce by associating equipment and safety. "When we talked about safety and how to keep this trip safe, we mentioned some of the special equipment we use canoeing, especially PFDs. All the equipment is important for a safe trip. Because of that, it is important to make sure all the equipment is working well. When we show you the equipment and how to use it, we'll also mention some tips on how to take care of it. We urge participants to follow the tips."

2. Introduce the "big 3" (canoe, paddle, and PFDs) and their parts.

   a. Canoes.
      1. Bow (front of a dog goes bow-wow; front of the canoe is the bow).
      2. Stern.
      3. Gunnels.
      4. Thwarts.
      5. Keel.
      6. Portage yolk.
      7. Seat.

   b. Paddles.
      1. Shaft.
      2. Blade of the paddle is like the blade of a knife.
      3. On land protect the blade of the paddle from sand and rocks.
      4. Rest it on your foot or something soft when you hold the paddle upright.
      5. Avoid banging paddle on the canoe deck.

   c. PFDs.
     1. Explain types.
       — Class One (those with seizure disorders must wear a Class One).
       — Class Two.
       — Class Three.
       — Class Five.
     2. Demonstrate sizing and how to put them on. "Always wear them. Avoid sand and abrasion. When you're not wearing them, put them someplace safe. They are not seat cushions. They can be used as pillows for your head. Sitting on them squishes the foam and takes the float out of them. Do not sit on PFDs."

3. Adaptive equipment.

   a. What it is.
     1. Sling seats.
     2. Crazy Creek chairs.
     3. Grips.
     4. One arm paddles.

   b. How it is used.

4. Safety equipment.

   a. Extra paddle.
   b. Repair kit.
   c. Throw rope.

5. Tip tests and rescues. Demonstrate tip test.

   a. Stay with the canoe.
   b. Talk; make sure everyone is OK.
   c. Turn canoe upright.
   d. Swim back into the canoe.
   e. Sit on the bottom.
   f. Paddle to shore.
   g. Empty the canoe; tip slowly so you do not have to lift lots of water.

E. Evaluation. Participants should be able to:

    1. Take care of the equipment.
    2. Understand the basic canoeing terminology used by staff members.
    3. Perform a tip test.

III. Packing the canoes.

A. Why? Participants should learn how to:

    1. Pack equipment so it stays dry.
    2. Pack equipment securely.
    3. Pack the canoes so they are well balanced.

B. When? Immediately before loading the canoes for the first time.

C. Methods: Demonstration and lecture.

D. Lesson.

    1. Plan a packing strategy.

        a. Put all that needs to go into the canoe in one place.
        b. This is important to see space and weight needs.
        c. Divide equipment into piles for each compartment based on space and weight.

    2. Load the canoe.
        a. Canoes should be in the still, shallow water. It is best if they are floating.
        b. Load equipment, keeping the weight balanced.
        c. Try to avoid packing so the bow is heavier than the stern, it is more difficult to steer. Keep canoe level or slightly down at the stern.
        d. Wheelchairs: Pack so the canoe is balanced and *tie all parts to the canoe.*

     3. Try to remember packing strategy.

  E. Evaluation: Canoes should be properly balanced when loaded.

IV. Paddling techniques.

  A. Why? Participants should be taught:

     1. How to hold the paddle.
     2. Basic strokes: forward stroke, J-stroke, draw, pry, reverse, and possibly sweep.

  B. When? Right before the first time participants paddle the canoes.
  C. Methods. Demonstration and lecture, if possible, on a sandy beach area.

  D. Lesson.

     1. Show how to hold the paddle.

       a. Finding the proper size paddle. Roughly stand the paddle upright in front of you, with the end of the blade resting on your toes. The handle should be between your chin and your nose.

       b. Proper placement of your hands. Stand the paddle upright in front of you, with the end of the blade resting on your toes. Put one hand on top of the paddle so you can wave your fingers away from you. With your other hand, grab the shaft of the paddle just above the blade. This puts hands in the proper position. Try to relax your grip on each stroke.

     2. Basic strokes. Demonstrate these, preferably using a long stick or paddle shaft to make the strokes in the sand; this makes the demonstration more visible to participants.

a. *Forward stroke.* Moves canoe forward.
   1. Reach paddle blade forward.
   2. Bury the blade in the water.
   3. Pull paddle blade toward the back of the canoe by dropping your top hand diagonally from shoulder level to waist level without really bending your elbow; turn your torso as your hand makes this motion or punch your top hand forward at shoulder level while pulling your level hand back to your waist.
   4. Recovery. Gently lift the blade out of the water, trying not to splash.
   Feather the paddle—turn the blade so it cuts the wind. Swing the paddle forward; you shouldn't need to lift the paddle far out of the water.
   5. The more water you move, the more you will move forward. Bury the blade in the water.
   6. Try to keep paddle blade close to the center line of the canoe or the canoe will turn.
   7. Use as much of your body as you can.
   8. Turn torso.
   9. Avoid banging paddle on the canoe deck.
   10. Death grips are tiring and unhealthy. Try to relax your grip on each stroke.
   11. Pace yourself. Try to find a rhythm as you would for a long bicycle ride.

b. *J-stroke.* Like the forward stroke, but add turn at the end.
   1. Turn your top wrist so your thumb points toward the water.
   2. Push the paddle blade away from the canoe.
   3. The push motion is what turns the canoe.
   4. Mastering the J-stroke is a balancing act between the power of the forward stroke and the strength of the turning motion. It takes practice.

c. *Draw (pull-to)*. Moves canoe sideways.
   1. Reach straight to the side.
   2. The whole paddle stays vertical.
   3. Bury the blade in the water, flat side facing you.
   4. Pull the blade toward you by pulling lower wrist to your waist and upper wrist toward your nose
   5. Recovery.
      — Underwater, turn wrist so paddle blade is at a right angle to the canoe. Push paddle away from canoe with the blade cutting the water.
      — Above water, lift the blade clear of the water. Reach far to the side of the canoe. Bury the blade in the water.

d. *Pry (push-away)*. It is the draw stroke in reverse, moves canoe sideways.
   1. The whole paddle stays vertical and the stroke is made to the side of the paddler.
   2. Bury the blade in the water, near the side of the canoe, flat side facing you.
   3. Push the blade away from you.
   4. Recovery.
      — Underwater, turn wrist so paddle blade is at a right angle to the canoe. Pull paddle toward the canoe with the blade cutting the water.
      — Above water, lift the blade clear of the water. Bring the paddle to the side of the canoe. Bury the blade in the water.

e. *Reverse*. Moves canoe backward or at least slows it down.
   1. Turn torso and look backward over your shoulder. Bury the paddle blade in the water by straightening your elbow and dropping your hand toward the water.
   2. Turn your torso (and straighten your elbow) to bring your hand and the paddle blade forward.

3. Keep your top hand near your shoulder throughout the stroke.
4. Recovery. Lift the paddle blade up and out of the water. Turn torso to move the paddle blade behind you. Now you are ready to bury the paddle blade behind you.

f. *Sweep.* Turns canoe.
    1. Like forward stroke, but blade stays near the surface of the water.
    2. Blade makes a sweep instead of staying near center line of the canoe.
    3. Motion is made by turning torso.

E. Evaluation. Participants should:

    1. Be able to execute the five basic strokes when verbally instructed to do so.
    2. Have some idea of how each stroke will move a canoe.

V. Launching and landing.

A. Why? Participants should know the theory behind landing and launching a canoe:

    1. Without flipping.
    2. Without damaging the canoe.

B. When? Before launching or landing for the first time.

C. Methods. Lecture and demonstration.

D. Lesson.

    1. Where to launch and land.

        a. Picking the right spot is key to making it easier—always look for potential landing spots.

    b. Things to look for.
      1.Wind-sheltered area.
      2.Beach.
      3.No "canoe-eating" rocks.

    c. Land before you really need to so you can be picky about where to land.

2. Launching techniques.

    a. Load the canoe, preferably floating in shallow water.

    b. Bow paddler gets into the canoe while the bow is floating.

    c. Stern paddler gets into the canoe, pushing the canoe away from the shallows.

    d. After launching, wait for the group to get into paddling formation.

3. Landing technique.

    a. Land one canoe at a time.

    b. Slow down as you approach the shore.

    c. Try to get out and stop the canoe before it hits the bottom or rocks.

    d. Hold the canoe stable as it floats until everyone is out.

    e. Keep the canoe floating until it is unloaded. One end can be rested on the ground to keep the canoe in place, but do not lift loaded canoes.

E. Evaluation. Participants should understand:

1. How to select good launching and landing sites.
2. How to make a safe landing.

Follow-up activities.

— Local canoe club.
— Local lakes, rivers, bays, and places to canoe.
— Local rental/retail outlets or dealers.
— Local camps and agencies with canoe programs or equipment.
— More advanced learning opportunities.
— Whitewater canoeing opportunities and instruction.
— Other learning opportunities.

Evaluation of learner outcomes.

1. Review each specific objective to determine if all learners have achieved these objectives.

2. Methods to evaluate include:
    — Observe participants performing activities.
    — Observe safety procedures used by participants.
    — Ask participants questions related to information given in lesson.
    — Ask participants for evaluative feedback.

Evaluation of teaching/lesson process.

1. Written evaluation of teaching process.
2. Verbal evaluation of teaching process.
3. Observation of participants performing the skills.
4. Unsolicited comments from participants, family, care providers, and staff members.

Fishing partners

Chapter Seven

A SYSTEMIC APPROACH TO MAKING OUTDOOR ENVIRONMENTS MORE INCLUSIONARY

In previous chapters, specific person-by-person or person-to-person strategies for integrated outdoor adventure programs were described. Unfortunately, however, it is not unusual for a highly successful integrated outdoor program to "self-destruct," perhaps because an enthusiastic program director leaves the agency. "Once integrated" does not necessarily mean "always integrated." What is needed, therefore, is a *systemic* approach, a *holistic* approach, an approach *relating agencies* while *cooperatively linking participants of varying abilities*, an approach that *builds a team of adult advocates*. In other words, a systemic approach requires interrelating concrete, applied, direct strategies with less direct, advocacy-oriented, process-oriented strategies.

Over the last 12 years, we have developed a framework that helps us to take a systemic approach to integrated outdoor activity (Figure 7.1). On the left side, adults are represented (*e.g.,* parents, outdoor educators, scout leaders) who provide the "spark" to ignite an integrated emphasis and then assume various roles to keep the "fire" going. Lines one and two, moving from left to right, show specific, concrete, direct strategies that adults can use to actively plan and promote integration (*e.g.,* preparing nondisabled peers to interact capably, or reinforcing

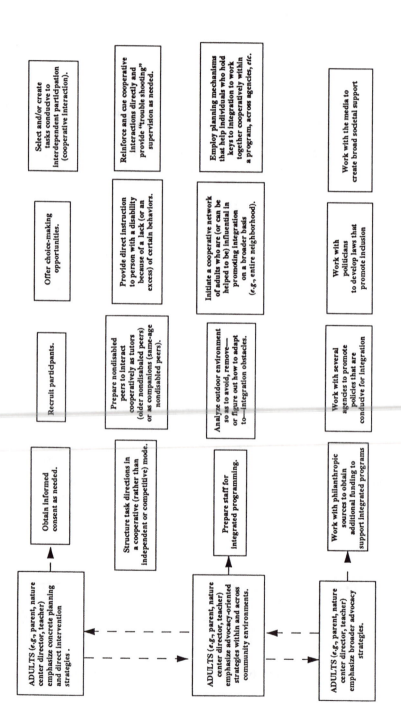

Figure 7.1. Promoting integration with a socialization emphasis. Based on Rynders & Schleien (1991).

cooperative interactions). The third line illustrates advocacy strategies that help adults to link agencies and key providers into supportive networks. Illustrative of this strategy is the Circle of Friends (O'Brien *et al.*, 1989; Chapter 4) that helps parents, peers, siblings, program leaders, and others work together on a plan to strengthen and enrich the life of a person who has a disability.

The fourth line depicts important, but relatively indirect, strategies of personal and political advocacy. Illustrative of this strategy is a parent who walks into the ski rental shop of the local park and requests that her child with severe vision impairments be given an opportunity to use the park's cross-country ski trails. Brushed aside verbally by the person in charge, the parent demands access to the park's policy statements. Finding no policy statements that relate to the situation, the parent organizes a policy development task force, ultimately presenting her case to the county park board. Soon thereafter, provisions are made for her daughter to ski with a sighted companion. Parenthetically, through the parent's efforts, not only is an individual with serious visual impairments skiing regularly with a sighted companion, the park has become more accommodative and park staff are more appreciative of ability diversities. Obviously, everyone has benefited. *Mutuality of benefit*, the essence of inclusionary excellence, can be expected from a successful, systemic, integrated experience.

Adults who are informed about and committed to integrated programs of the highest quality are the "moving force" that make a systemic approach successful. In terms of Figure 7.1, adult intervention can begin at all levels together or at any level individually. A systemic approach—if it is to be successful— must ultimately have productive activity at all levels—from the broadest to narrowest, from the most direct to least direct, and from both a product and process standpoint.

Are there examples of integrated outdoor adventure programs that have sustained high quality for extended time periods using a systemic approach to programming? Wilderness Inquiry (WI) and the Bloomington Park and Recreation Division are examples of agencies with such programs in Minnesota.

Wilderness Inquiry

Greg Lais, WI's director, maintains a consistent overall emphasis on integrated wilderness experiences. All trips, without exception, are planned to include persons with and without disabilities. Recently, 10 adults without disabilities (including one personal care attendant, seven paying participants, and two WI staff) and three adults with disabilities went on a trip to the Boundary Waters Canoe Area Wilderness (BWCAW) in northern Minnesota. Tim, a person with serious language and mobility problems due to cerebral palsy, required a personal care attendant for assistance in eating, dressing, toileting, and self-care tasks. Jennifer, also using a wheelchair, had been injured in an auto accident that paralyzed her lower limbs but allowed normal use of her upper limbs. Pat had no mobility problems but was moderately mentally retarded and socially withdrawn.

Reflecting lines one and two of Figure 7.1, sling-seat modifications in a canoe allowed Jennifer to paddle even though she could not support herself upright on the standard canoe seat. Tim could not move across rocky and muddy portage trails in his wheelchair with any degree of independence; but he could be "walked" across the portage by his attendant, preserving Tim's motivation to participate. Around the campfire Pat stirred the vegetable stew, although he could not slice up the vegetables. The cooperatively created stew rewarded each person with a delicious meal.

When setting up tents, teams of participants with and without disabilities worked together, allowing partial participation of two or three campers. When it was time to tip the canoe to practice water safety procedures, it required a great deal of courage for Tim to rely on his flotation device (and staff and companions if necessary) to keep him from drowning. But, working together, Tim and his canoeing partners survived (and even relished) the dunking.

Other WI inclusionary strategies (reflected in the third line of Figure 7.1) are less direct but are essential in achieving a systemic outcome. At WI's inception, few outdoor educators believed that people with serious disabilities could access the BWCAW, since it presents serious challenges to physically fit and wilderness-experienced individuals. But, the WI staff analyzed the environments they wished to tackle on an integrated basis, planning how obstacles could be avoided, overcome, or handled to allow both independence and positive interdependence. Titanium wheelchairs with oversize wheels replaced typical wheelchairs, so that persons using them could move across portage trails, with nondisabled companions assisting in some cases or simply acting as spotters in others. No adaptations or modest adaptations were preferred over substantial adaptations to preserve a normalized experience that was safe and motivating.

Policy-driven strategies (fourth line of Figure 7.1) show up in WI's efforts to influence national legislation, legislation that is already providing fuller access to America's wilderness areas by persons of varying abilities.

Overcoming challenges—A matter of attitude.

Bloomington Park and Recreation Division

Bloomington Park and Recreation has conducted integrated programs for several years, although it also provides segregated options. Jason, a child with multiple disabilities, has attended the program regularly for three years.

Jason was 11 years old when he attended a self-contained, segregated classroom for children with severe and multiple disabilities. His mother was preparing to integrate Jason into the neighborhood middle school; her greatest fear was that Jason would not get to know the other children. She deemed socialization to be his greatest need. She believed that a path to success in his integration at school would be to help him build relationships—preferably, friendships—before the fall term. To assess Jason's current relationships and friendships, his mother and a certified therapeutic recreation specialist constructed a Circle of Friends diagram (Schleien *et al.*, 1990; Chapter 4).

Only two same-age peers appeared on Jason's initial circle. One was a boy who lived about three blocks away and visited him periodically. Jason did not see him outside of these visits. The second was a rotating "special friend" who helped in the special education classroom. These peers were placed on Jason's outer circle because of their transient roles in his life. This procedure documented Jason's need to build friendships with other children and became the focus of Jason's outdoor program during the summer. To offer Jason and his neighborhood peers an opportunity to get to know one another, several long-term social outdoor education/recreation programs were selected for Jason's integrative participation. The programs included a supervised eight-week outdoor program at a neighborhood park and a two-week day camp.

Careful planning, communication, and support building were undertaken by Jason's parents, the therapeutic recreation specialist/integration facilitator, outdoor educator, aides, park and recreation supervisors, and site personnel. Formal and informal environmental assessments, outdoor education/leisure interest assessments, and skill inventories were completed. Staff were trained. A companionship training program with a cooperative learning orientation was conducted and the second phase of the Circle of Friends was initiated. This phase involved the outdoor education and camp participants in the process of integrating

Jason into the program. Jason was introduced by the outdoor educator as an 11-year-old boy who lived in a nearby neighborhood; he would be attending fifth grade at the middle school in the fall. And he wished to participate in the outdoor activities. A photo album was shared to give the children without disabilities an opportunity to see the activities that Jason and his family enjoy.

The outdoor educator and park staff were apprehensive that the summer program might not be a success for everyone. The nondisabled participants were asked why they thought that the adults were uneasy about Jason joining the program. The children responded with, "We may tease or ignore Jason." Then they were asked, "What are the things you can do to make this program a success?" They responded, "We can say hello, invite Jason to play, talk with him, and show him how we play the games." The outdoor educator followed this introduction with the MAPS questions and discussion areas (*i.e.*, dreams, nightmares, likes, strengths, and needs) (see Chapter 4). The answers that Jason's parents and siblings provided previously were shared. This discussion empowered the participants to contribute to the program's success.

The next step was to structure interactions for cooperative learning. The staff was responsible for structuring activities, learning how to promote interdependence (cooperation), learning when and how to cue and reinforce positive interactions, developing an understanding of how and when to redirect activities, and understanding that rapid intervention would be necessary if a situation became unsafe. The aide who assisted Jason was responsible for his personal needs (*i.e.*, toileting, feeding, and movement) and for attempting to facilitate interactions between Jason and his peers. Peers without disabilities had their general friendship skills sharpened (*e.g.*, "Friends take turns, smile at each other, and stay close when playing together"), and also learned how to be a companion when that was appropriate. They learned when and how to model and/or physically guide a response when Jason indicated that he did not know what to do. They also learned basic manual communication signs that Jason used.

Throughout the summer, program leaders encouraged the children to make suggestions and adaptations and to create games in which everyone could participate. By the end of summer, it was the consensus of the staff and Jason's aide that the children had invented more creative ways than did the adults to include Jason and make it fun for everyone. To evaluate Jason's progress, another Circle of Friends diagram was constructed, revealing increased and/or richer social relationships. The summer was a success for everyone.

Experiences of inclusion continued for Jason, as a team of adults, led by his parents, continued to work together. In the fall, he was welcomed by his outdoor education group and camp friends at his school, where a Circle of Friends procedure continued to assist in his integration. During the following summer, he was joined daily by a friend who lived down the street. Jason was often invited to his home for snacks and to play; he even joined his new friend and his family on a camping trip. When he was introduced at a day camp program the following summer, 10 of 18 campers listed Jason on their Circle of Friends diagrams before the program commenced.

Not all integrated outdoor education/adventure programs are as successful as those conducted by Wilderness Inquiry and Bloomington Park and Recreation. When integrated programs disintegrate (often reverting to a former segregated model), it is almost always due to an incomplete or poorly articulated set of systemic components and/or a lack of committed and skilled adults to maintain a strong advocacy role.

Two examples of integration disintegration can be seen in a camping program and a nature center program, both of which had been integrated successfully and were deemed able to sustain the integrated effort—only to revert to a segregated pattern when the temporary help from our research team was discontinued.

The integrated camping program was begun after more than two decades of strong segregated programming. The camp director was committed to integration and invited our team to prepare his staff for integration. After two weeks of round-the-clock integrated camping, participants without disabilities displayed a significant improvement in attitude toward people with disabilities and in their own self-esteem; participants with disabilities made excellent progress in developing better camping skills; staff members rated the experience as significantly better than the former segregated one (though they remarked that it was more difficult to conduct an integrated camp program). But, the program collapsed when we left. Why? The philanthropic foundation supporting the camp apparently was not sold on integration (their mission statement remained unchanged). Furthermore, some influential staff members had so many years of segregated camping experience that it was difficult for them to break out of that pattern.

The nature center project involved integrating children with Down syndrome with nondisabled, same-age partners. The task of choice was snowshoeing. At the outset, the director and her staff were trained to conduct integrated programming, that is, they learned how to prepare nondisabled peers to be cooperative partners, learned how to structure snowshoeing as a cooperative task, *etc.* Our staff supplied modified snowshoes and suggested task modifications to make the use of snowshoes easier for participants with Down syndrome. Integrated successfully for two months, one year later, the nature center program did not display any evidence of integration. Why not? Adults who needed to sustain the effort reported that the continued use of modified snowshoes was problematic because of the longer time required to fasten them on, *etc.*, creating scheduling problems. Moreover, some of the adults said that modifying snowshoes and adapted snowshoeing was too intrusive for neighborhood people (who were, of course, able to use snowshoes without modifications).

In both these cases, the collapse of the integrated program was caused by a break down in the active support of key adults, individuals who could energize, advocate, plan, and maintain an integrated program effectively.

Traits of a High-quality Integrated Program

In closing, we believe that it is important to share a vision for the future that complements the content of Figure 7.1. It takes the form of a checklist of quality indicators, addressing the question: "What signs can I look for in identifying an integrated outdoor education program of high quality for a person with a disability?" The following list of quality indicators for an outdoor education and high adventure program was developed at the University of Minnesota (Schleien & Kuhnly, 1989).

ADMINISTRATION

— Statement of mission/philosophy and policies reflect a strong belief in social integration.

— Staff hiring criteria give credit for education and/or experience with integration.

— Adherence (preferably enthusiastic adherence) to laws and legislation pertaining to serving persons with disabilities in least restrictive environments is apparent in the personnel office, *etc.*

— Staff training priorities emphasize regularly scheduled continuing education opportunities in topical areas such as innovations and techniques in integration, use of community-based consultants, *etc.*

— Documentation of integration services/interventions is provided and effects on participants are recorded in logs or other evaluative instruments.

NATURE OF PROGRAM

— Features integrated programs but may provide segregated programs as integration "stepping stones" (allows for choice).

— Provides flexible programs, allowing for ongoing modifications and adaptations (*e.g.,* partial participation), if needed.

— Program goals reflect an active inclusionary emphasis, such as interdependent activity provisions, friend-oriented interaction modes, *etc.*

ACTIVITIES

— Are chronologically age-appropriate, functional, and have lifelong learning potential.

— Can be generalized across time, environments, and people.

— Allow for personal challenge ("dignity of risk") and personal choice but without sacrificing necessary participatory safeguards.

ENVIRONMENTAL/LOGISTICAL CONSIDERATIONS

— Environment is physically accessible. If an environment is not accessible (*e.g.*, a remote wilderness area), staff members work with all participants to provide an appropriate substitution or modified access.

— Programming is offered at a convenient time for participants.

— Cost is reasonable and sponsorships are available.

TECHNIQUES AND METHODS

— Appropriate involvement of unpaid or paid partners is made available.

— Ongoing assessments are conducted of participants' outdoor education and recreation needs, preferences, choices, skills, and enjoyment levels.

— Parents/careproviders and consumers are included in assessment, program planning, and evaluation activities.

— Integration techniques, such as cooperative learning, environmental analysis, partial participation, trainer advocacy, and companionship training are employed regularly and skillfully.

— Ongoing program evaluation is conducted to make programming adaptations as needed.

The time has come to assume a new way of thinking, one that is founded on the premise that the outdoors belong to everyone and everyone belongs to the outdoors. Strong, integrated, outdoor education and high adventure programs are ideal vehicles for promoting this new way of thinking.

Social integration—What it is all about.

Bibliography

Chapter 1

Dattilo, J. and Murphy, W.D. (1987). Facilitating the challenge in adventure recreation for persons with disabilities. *Therapeutic Recreation Journal*, 21(3), 14-21.

Ewert, A.W. (1989). *Outdoor Adventure Pursuits: Foundations, Models, and Theories*. Columbus, OH: Publishing Horizons.

Ford, P. (1980). *Principles and Practices of Outdoor/Environmental Education*. New York: John Wiley.

Gibson, P. (1979). Therapeutic aspects of wilderness programs: A comprehensive literature review. *Therapeutic Recreation Journal*, 8(2), 21-33.

Hornfeldt, D.A., McAvoy, L.H., and Schleien, S.J. (1989). Influences of integration on learning of natural history concepts by children with and without disabilities. In M.H. Legg (Ed.), *Proceedings of the Research Symposiums: 1989 National Association of Interpretation Workshop* (pp. 408-415). Fort Collins, CO: National Association of Interpretation.

Lais, G. (1987). Toward fullest participation—Suggested leadership techniques for integrated adventure programming. *Bradford Papers Annual*, 2, 55-64.

McAvoy, L.H. (1987). The experiential components of a high-adventure program. In J.F. Meier, T.W. Morash, and G.E. Welton (Eds.), *High Adventure Outdoor Pursuits* (pp. 200-209). Columbus, OH: Publishing Horizons.

McAvoy, L.H. and Schleien, S.J. (1988). Effects of integrated interpretive programs on persons with and without disabilities. In L.A. Beck (Ed.), *Research in Interpretation: Proceedings of the 1988 National Association of Interpretation Research Symposium* (pp. 13-26). San Diego, CA: Institute for Leisure Behavior, San Diego State University.

McAvoy, L.H., Schatz, E.C., Stutz, M.E., Schleien, S.J., and Lais, G. (1989). Integrated wilderness adventure: Effects on personal and lifestyle traits of persons with and without disabilities. *Therapeutic Recreation Journal*, 23(3), 51-64.

Robb, G.M. and Ewert, A. (1987). Risk recreation and persons with disabilities. *Therapeutic Recreation Journal*, 21(1), 58-69.

Robb, G.M., Havens, M.D., and Witman, J.P. (1983). *Special Education...Naturally*. Bloomington: Indiana University.

Schleien, S.J. and Ray, M.T. (1988). *Community Recreation and Persons with Disabilities: Strategies for Integration*. Baltimore: Paul H. Brookes.

Wolfensberger, W. (1972). *Normalization: The Principle of Normalization in Human Services*. Toronto: National Institute on Mental Retardation.

Chapter 2

Brannan, S.A., Roland, C., Smith, T., and Rillo, T. (1984). Current issues in camping and outdoor education with persons who are disabled. *The Bradford Papers*, 4, 1-5.

Farbman, A.H. and Ellis, W.K. (1987). Accessibility and outdoor recreation for persons with disabilities. *Therapeutic Recreation Journal*, 21(1), 70-76.

Lais, G.L., Ellis, W.K., and Galland, J.H. (1990). Access to wilderness by persons with disabilities. In D.W. Lime (Ed.), *Managing America's Enduring Wilderness Resource* (pp. 243-249). St. Paul: Minnesota Extension Service, University of Minnesota.

McAvoy, L. (1982). Management components in therapeutic outdoor adventure programs. *Therapeutic Recreation Journal*, 16(4), 13-20.

McAvoy, L.H., Dustin, D.L., Rankin, J., and Frakt, A. (1985). Wilderness and legal liability: Guidelines for resource managers and program leaders. *Journal of Park and Recreation Administration*, 3(1), 41-49.

Peterson, C. (1978). The right to risk. *Journal of Physical Education and Recreation*. April, 23-24.

Priest, S. and Dixon, T. (1990). *Safety Practices in Adventure Programming*. Boulder, CO: Association for Experiential Education.

Schleien, S.J., Ray, M.T., and Johnson, D. (1989). An architectural accessibility survey of community recreation centers. *Journal of Park and Recreation Administration*, 7(3), 10-22.

van der Smissen, B. (1979). Minimizing legal liability risks. *Journal of Experiential Education*. Spring, 35-41.

van der Smissen, B. (1990). *Legal Liability and Risk Management for Public and Private Entities.* Cincinnati, OH: Anderson.

Chapter 3

Lais, G. (1987). Toward fullest participation—Suggested leadership techniques for integrated adventure programming. *Bradford Papers Annual*, 2, 55-64.

McAvoy, L. (1982). Management components in therapeutic outdoor adventure programs. *Therapeutic Recreation Journal*, 16(4), 13-20.

Stitch, T.F. and Gaylor, M.S. (1984). Risk management in adventure programs with special populations. *Journal of Experiential Education*, 7(3), 15-19.

Chapter 4

Amado, R. (1988). Behavioral principles in community recreation integration. In S. Schleien and M.T. Ray (Eds.), *Community Recreation and Persons with Disabilities: Strategies for Integration* (pp. 79-90). Baltimore: Paul H. Brookes.

Anderson, S.C., and Allen, L.R. (1985). Effects of a leisure education program on activity involvement and social interaction of mentally retarded persons. *Adapted Physical Activity Quarterly*, 2(2), 107-116.

Banks, R. and Aveno, A. (1986). Adapted miniature golf: A community leisure program for students with severe physical disabilities. *Journal of the Association for Persons with Severe Handicaps*, 11, 209-215.

Baumgart, D., Brown, L., Pumpian, I., Nisbet, J., Ford, A., Sweet, M., Messina, R., and Schroeder, J. (1982). Principle of partial participation and individualized adaptations in educational programs for severely handicapped students. *Journal of the Association for Persons with Severe Handicaps*, 8(3), 71-77.

Certo, N.J., Schleien, S.J., and Hunter, D. (1983). An ecological assessment inventory to facilitate community recreation participation by severely disabled individuals. *Therapeutic Recreation Journal,* 17(3), 29-38.

Dattilo, J. (1991). Mental retardation. In D. Austin and M. Crawford (Eds.), *Therapeutic Recreation: An Introduction* (pp. 163-188). Englewood Cliffs, NJ: Prentice Hall.

Dattilo, J. and Mirenda, P. (1987). The application of a leisure preference assessment protocol for persons with severe handicaps. *Journal of the Association for Persons with Severe Handicaps,* 12(4), 306-311.

Dattilo, J. and Murphy, W. (1987). *Behavior Modification in Therapeutic Recreation.* State College, PA: Venture.

Dattilo, J. and Murphy, W. (1991). *Leisure Education Program Planning: A Systematic Approach.* State College, PA: Venture.

Deutsch, M. (1962). Cooperation and trust: Some theoretical notes. In M.R. Jones (Ed.), *Nebraska Symposium on Motivation* (pp. 275-320). Lincoln: University of Nebraska Press.

Ford, A., Brown, L., Pumpian, I., Baumgart, D., Nisbet, J., Schroeder, J., and Loomis, R. (1984). Strategies for developing individual recreation/leisure plans for adolescent and young adult severely handicapped students. In N. Certo, N. Haring, and R. York (Eds.), *Public School Integration of Severely Handicapped Students: Rational Issues and Progressive Alternatives* (pp. 245-275). Baltimore: Paul H. Brookes.

Green, F.P. (1982). Outdoor recreation for the physically disabled. *Selected Proceedings of the 32nd Annual National Intramural-Recreational Sports Conference,* 32, 157-163.

Hoops, H. (1981). Tips for environmental education: Working with special audiences. *Nature Study,* 34(3), 14-15, 17.

Johnson, D.W. and Johnson, F.P. (1987). *Joining Together: Group Theory and Group Skills.* Englewood Cliffs, NJ: Prentice-Hall.

Johnson, D.W. and Johnson, R.T. (1975). *Learning Together and Alone: Cooperation, Competition, and Individualization.* Englewood Cliffs, NJ: Prentice-Hall.

Katz, G. and Bushnell, S. (1979). Meeting special needs through environmental education. *Teaching Exceptional Children,* 11, 110-113.

Lais, G. (1988). *Wilderness Inquiry Staff Manual.* Minneapolis: Wilderness Inquiry.

Lakin, K.C. and Bruininks, R.H. (1985). *Strategies for Achieving Community Integration of Developmentally Disabled Citizens.* Baltimore: Paul H. Brookes.

Lanagan, D. and Dattilo, J. (1989). The effects of a leisure education program on individuals with mental retardation. *Therapeutic Recreation Journal,* 23(4), 62-72.

Nietupski, J., Hamre-Nietupski, S., and Ayres, B. (1984). Review of task analytic leisure skill training efforts: Practitioner implications and future research needs. *Journal of the Association for Persons with Severe Handicaps,* 9, 88-97.

O'Brien, J., Forest, M., Snow, J., and Hasbury, D. (1989). *Action for Inclusion: How to Improve Schools by Welcoming Children With Special Needs into Regular Classrooms.* Toronto: Centre for Integrated Education, Frontier College.

Perske, R. and Perske, M. (1988). *Circle of Friends: People with Disabilities and Their Friends Enrich the Lives of One Another.* Nashville: Abingdon.

Ray, M.T., Schleien, S.J., Larson, A., Rutten, T., and Slick, C. (1986). Integrating persons with disabilities into community leisure environments. *Journal of Expanding Horizons in Therapeutic Recreation,* 1(1), 49-55.

Richardson, D., Wilson, B., Wetherald, L., and Peters, J. (1987). Mainstreaming initiative: An innovative approach to recreation and leisure services in a community setting. *Therapeutic Recreation Journal,* 21(2), 9-19.

Robb, G.M. (1984). Outdoor education—An alternative to learning for children with special needs. *The Bradford Papers,* 4, 49-53.

Rynders, J. and Schleien, S. (1991). *Together Successfully: Creating Recreational and Educational Programs That Integrate People with and without Disabilities.* Arlington, TX: Association for Retarded Citizens-United States, National 4-H, and the Institute on Community Integration, University of Minnesota.

Rynders, J.E., Schleien, S.J., and Mustonen, T. (1990). Integrating children with severe disabilities for intensified outdoor education: Focus on feasibility. *Mental Retardation,* 28, 7-14.

Rynders, J., Johnson, R., Johnson, D., and Schmidt, B. (1980). Producing positive interaction among Down syndrome and nonhandicapped teenagers through cooperative goal structuring. *American Journal of Mental Deficiency,* 85, 268-273.

Schleien, S. (1991). Severe multiple disabilities. *In* D. Austin and M. Crawford (Eds.), *Therapeutic Recreation: An Introduction* (pp. 189-223). Englewood Cliffs, NJ: Prentice Hall.

Schleien, S.J., Fahnestock, M., Green, R., and Rynders, J.E. (1990). Building positive social networks through environmental interventions in integrated recreation programs. *Therapeutic Recreation Journal*, 24(4), 42-52.

Schleien, S., Olson, K., Rogers, N., and McLafferty, M. (1985). Integrating children with severe handicaps into recreation and physical education programs. *Journal of Park and Recreation Administration*, 3(1), 50-66.

Schleien, S. and Ray, M.T. (1988). *Community Recreation and Persons with Disabilities: Strategies for Integration.* Baltimore: Paul H. Brookes.

Schleien, S., Rynders, J., Mustonen, J., and Fox, A. (1990). Effects of social play activities on the play behavior of children with autism. *Journal of Leisure Research*, 22, 317-328.

Vandercook, T. and York, J. (1989). The McGill Action Planning System (MAPS): A strategy for building the vision. *Journal of the Association for Persons with Severe Handicaps*, 14, 205-215.

Voeltz, L., Hempill, N., Brown, S., Kishi, R., Fruehling, R., Levy, G., Collie, J., and Kube, C. (1983). *The Special Friends Program: A Trainers Manual for Integrated School Settings* (rev. ed.). Honolulu: University of Hawaii.

Wehman, P. and Moon, M.S. (1985). Designing and implementing leisure programs for individuals with severe handicaps. In M.P. Brady and P.L. Gunter (Eds.), *Integrating Moderately and Severely Handicapped Learners: Strategies That Work* (pp. 214-237). Springfield, IL: Charles C. Thomas.

Wehman, P. and Schleien, S. (1980). Assessment and selection of leisure skills for severely handicapped individuals. *Education and Training of the Mentally Retarded*, 15, 50-57.

Wehman, P. and Schleien, S. (1981). *Leisure Programs for Handicapped Persons: Adaptations, Techniques, and Curriculum.* Austin, TX: Pro-Ed.

Wehman, P., Schleien, S., and Kiernan, J. (1980). Age appropriate recreation programs for severely handicapped youth and adults. *Journal of the Association for the Severely Handicapped*, 5, 395-407.

Wuerch, B.B. , and Voeltz, L.M. (1982). *Longitudinal Leisure Skills for Severely Handicapped Learners: The Ho'onanea Curriculum Component.* Baltimore: Paul H. Brookes.

Chapter 5

American National Red Cross. (1977). *Adapted Aquatics: Swimming for Persons with Physical or Mental Impairments.* Garden City, NY: Doubleday.

Calculator, S. and Dollaghan, C. (1982). The use of communications boards in a residential setting: An evaluation. *Journal of Speech and Hearing Disorders,* 47, 281-287.

Dattilo, J. and Camarata, S. (1988). Combining speech pathology and therapeutic recreation to encourage self-determination for persons with disabilities. *Journal of Expanding Horizons in Therapeutic Recreation,* 3, 12-17.

Dixon, J. (1981). *Adapting Activities for Therapeutic Recreation Services: Concepts and Applications.* San Diego: Campanile.

Goldenson, R., Dunham, J., and Dunham, C. (1978). *Disability and Rehabilitation Handbook.* New York: McGraw-Hill.

Hamre-Nietupski, S., Nietupski, J., Sandvig, R., Sandvig, M.B., and Ayres, B. (1984). Leisure skills instruction in a community residential setting with young adults who are deaf/blind severely handicapped. *Journal of the Association for Persons with Severe Handicaps,* 9, 49-53.

Heyne, L. (1987). *Integrating Children and Youth With Disabilities into Community Recreation Agencies: One Agency's Experience and Recommendations.* St. Paul, MN: Jewish Community Center of the Greater St. Paul Area.

Heyne, L. and Schleien, S. (in press). Leisure and recreation programming to enhance quality of life. In E. Cipani and F. Spooner (Eds.), *Curricular and Instructional Approaches for Persons with Severe Handicaps.* Boston: Allyn and Bacon.

Lais, G. (1988). *Wilderness Inquiry Staff Manual.* Minneapolis: Wilderness Inquiry.

Realon, R.E., Flavell, J.E., and Phillips, J.F. (1989). Adapted leisure materials vs. standard leisure materials: Evaluating several aspects of programming for persons who are profoundly handicapped. *Education and Training in Mental Retardation,* 24(2), 168-177.

Schleien, S., Ash, T., Kiernan, J., and Wehman, P. (1981). Developing independent cooking skills in a profoundly retarded woman. *Journal of the Association for the Severely Handicapped*, 6(2), 23-29.

Schleien, S.J., Certo, N.J., and Muccino, A. (1984). Acquisition of leisure skills by a severely handicapped adolescent: A data based instructional program. *Education and Training of the Mentally Retarded*, 19(4), 297-305.

Schleien, S., Kiernan, J., and Wehman, P. (1981). Evaluation of an age-appropriate leisure skills program for moderately retarded adults. *Education and Training of the Mentally Retarded*, 16(1), 13-19.

Schleien, S., Light, C., McAvoy, L., and Baldwin, C. (1989). Best professional practices: Serving persons with severe multiple disabilities. *Therapeutic Recreation Journal*, 23(3), 27-40.

Stolov, W. and Clowers, M. (1981). *Handbook of Severe Disability*. Washington, DC: Rehabilitation Services Administration, U.S. Department of Education.

Wehman, P. and Schleien, S. (1981). *Leisure Programs for Handicapped Persons: Adaptations, Techniques, and Curriculum*. Austin, TX: Pro-Ed.

Wuerch, B.B. and Voeltz, L.M. (1982). *Longitudinal Leisure Skills for Severely Handicapped Learners: The Ho'onanea Curriculum Component*. Baltimore: Paul H. Brookes.

Chapter 7

Bruininks, R.H., Thurlow, M.L., Lewis, D., and Larson, N. (1989). *Post-school Outcomes for Special Education Students and Other Students over One to Eight Years after High School*. Minneapolis: Institute on Community Integration, Department of Educational Psychology, University of Minnesota.

O'Brien, J., Forest, M., Snow, J., and Hasbury, D. (1989). *Action for Inclusion: How to Improve Schools by Welcoming Children with Special Needs into Regular Classrooms*. Toronto: Centre for Integrated Education, Frontier College.

Rynders, J. and Schleien, S. (1991). *Together Successfully: Creating Recreational and Educational Programs That Integrate People with and without Disabilities*. Arlington, TX: Association for Retarded Citizens-United States, National 4-H, and the Institute on Community Integration, University of Minnesota.

Schleien, S. and Kuhnly, K. (1989). Integrated community recreation: A search for quality. In S. Schleien and J. Rynders (Eds.), *IMPACT: Feature Issue on Integrated Leisure and Recreation,* p.3. Minneapolis: Institute on Community Integration, University of Minnesota.

Schleien, S. and Ray, M.T. (1988). *Community Recreation and Persons with Disabilities: Strategies for Integration.* Baltimore: Paul H. Brookes.

Schleien, S. and Werder, J. (1985). Perceived responsibilities of special recreation services in Minnesota. *Therapeutic Recreation Journal,* 19(3), 51-62.

Schleien, S., Fahnestock, M., Green, R., and Rynders, J. (1990). Building positive social networks through environmental interventions in integrated recreation programs. *Therapeutic Recreation Journal,* 24(4), 42-52.

Turnbull, A.P. and Turnbull, H.R. (1985). Developing independence. *Journal of Adolescent Health Care,* 6, 108-115.

Wuerch, B. B., and Voeltz, L. M. (1982). *Longitudinal Leisure Skills for Severely Handicapped Learners: The Ho'onanea Curriculum Component.* Baltimore: Paul H. Brookes.

Appendix A

Water Safety Policies for Outdoor Programs

Drowning and hypothermia are the primary killers in the wilderness. *Never underestimate the power of water.* These policies must be strictly enforced.

1. Participants should always be advised of their roles and responsibilities in the event of emergency. Participants shall be responsible first and foremost for their own safety, second for the safety of their group members, and last and least for the protection of food and equipment. Participants shall never be required to risk death or injury in the event of an emergency.

2. Water safety procedures and rules must be discussed at the beginning of each outdoor water program and trip.

3. *Everyone must wear an adequate personal flotation device (PFD) at all times while on the water. This must be checked and emphasized regularly.*
   A PFD must be buoyant enough to ensure a participant's head remains above water while floating free from a water craft. This system shall be arranged and tested on each participant at the beginning of the program, and it should include precautions for all states that the participant may encounter (*i.e.*, mobility impairments, black-outs, seizures, insulin shock, and bee sting allergies).
   If the person has a history of uncontrolled seizures in the previous two years, or if their body shape is such that they do not float in a regular vest, they shall be required to wear the maximum protection necessary to safeguard against acci-

dental drowning. They should wear a Class One or equivalent life vest. Always double check anyone who is wearing a Class One vest to make sure it is worn correctly.

4. No jumping or diving in the water is permitted.

5. Shoes must be worn at all times—in and out of the water. Some people resist this policy; however, it must be strictly enforced. Many people gash their feet on glass, rocks, cans, hooks, *etc*. At best, a foot injury disables the participant, and at worst, it requires evacuation.

6. If participants want to swim without their life jackets, leaders must first assess each person's swimming ability. Strict adherence to swim test standards must be observed—many people have trouble with and fail the swim test while wearing shoes. Adequate precaution to safeguard against accidents must be taken. If in doubt, do not allow a person to swim without a PFD. Swimming with shoes is meant to build respect for the water.

    Persons who experience seizures or who otherwise would be at risk without their life jackets must always wear their PFDs while swimming. To avoid social stratification, it is best to encourage everyone to keep their life jackets on while in the water.

7. Swimmers must be instructed to always use the "buddy" system. When people are swimming, one certified leader must be present to observe them in the water and have a canoe and PFDs ready for rescue.

8. Distance swimming is not allowed.

9. Participants may not swim without the consent of the leaders.

Appendix B

Participant Application, Health, and Assumption of Risk Form

Wilderness Inquiry Trip Application Form

RETURN COMPLETED FORM TO:
Wilderness Inquiry
1313 Fifth Street S.E., Suite 327
Minneapolis, MN 55414
612/379-3858 (Voice or TTY)

FOR OFFICE USE ONLY
Card sent____Confirmed_____
I.S._____Date_____

Name_____Date of Birth_____F___M__

Address_____

City_____ST_____Zip Code_____

Phone (day)_____(evening)_____
      (Please include area code)

TRIP DATE DESIRED: Please read the enclosed information and trip descriptions. Then list all possible trip choices in order of preference.

1st Choice_____2nd Choice_____3rd Choice_____

I am very flexible on dates_____Comments:_____

How did you hear about Wilderness Inquiry?_____

How many times have you been to the wilderness and on what kind of trips?_____

HEALTH INFORMATION: Having a disability does not disqualify anyone from the trips, but we do need to be aware of any special health care needs you may have. Please answer all questions thoroughly. Attach a separate note if you need more room.

Do you have any sensory, physical, cognitive or emotional disabilities? _____ If so, list and state how they

affect you. Please be explicit!_____

_____

What is your exact weight?_____What is your height?_____Can you walk unassisted on uneven terrain?___

Do you use a wheelchair ? _____Do you use crutches?_____Do you use a cane?_____If you have a disability, do you normally utilize the services of an attendant when:

_____eating?_____toileting?_____dressing?   Do you use a catheter?_____

Have you had any seizures in last two years? _____Do you take any medications to control seizures? _____
Are you currently taking prescription medications for any health problems? If yes, please list them and describe what they are for (attach separate sheet if necessary):

_____

Are you currently under the care of any medical specialists? If yes, for what conditions?_____

_____

Do you have any food allergies or dietary restrictions?_____ If yes, please describe:_____

_____

Have you had a tetanus shot in the last 4 years?____Yes____No

Have you experienced any of the following:

____Hemophilia   ____Allergic to bee stings   ____Allergic to penicillin
____Diabetes   ____Any other Allergies   ____Ear/throat infections
____Back conditions   ____Ear perforation   ____Dysreflexia
____Hernia/ruptures   ____Pressure sores   ____Heart defect/disease
____Kidney stones/infections ____Knee conditions   ____Chemical dependency
____Urinary/bladder infections ____Head aches   ____Lung disease
____Arthritis   ____Mental illness   ____Communicable diseases
____Bowel/bladder control problems

If you answered yes to any of the above, please describe more fully here:_____

_____

REFERENCES AND EMERGENCY INFORMATION:

Your health insurance company:_____policy #_____

Physician :_____(phone):_____
         (include area code)

Relative or close friend:_____Relationship:_____

Address:_____City_____ State____ Zip_____

Day Phone_____Evening Phone_____
              (include area code)

WE ASK THAT YOU READ AND SIGN THE FOLLOWING:

RELEASE OF LIABILITY: I recognize that there is a significant element of risk in any adventure sport or activity associated with the outdoors. Knowing of the inherent risks, dangers and rigors involved, I certify that I and/or my family (including any minor children), are fully capable of participating in the activities. I assume full responsibility for myself and/or my family, including any minor children, for bodily injury, death, loss of personal property and expenses thereof, as a result of my participation in a Wilderness Inquiry adventure. I have read, understand, and accept the terms and conditions stated herein and acknowledge that this agreement shall be effective and binding upon me during the entire period of participation in Wilderness Inquiry activities. I give permission for Wilderness Inquiry to check with my references and ask them questions regarding my participation in a Wilderness Inquiry adventure. I further give my permission for Wilderness Inquiry to use photographs taken of me on this trip for their promotional purposes.

Signed:_____ Date:_____

This form must be signed. If you are under 21, or if you are considered a vulnerable adult, your legal guardian must sign it.

THANK YOU FOR YOUR INTEREST IN WILDERNESS INQUIRY.
We will do our best to confirm your participation soon.   Revised 3/14/89

Appendix C

Outdoor Education Accessibility Survey

Development

The Outdoor Education Accessibility Survey is based on a survey developed by the Minnesota State Council for the Handicapped (Metro Square, 7th and Robert St., Suite 208, St. Paul, MN) and revised (in 1985) by the Project for Integrated Recreation in the Community (PIRC). In 1986, staff from the Therapeutic Recreation-Outdoor Education (TR-OE) Grant Project added items endemic to nature centers, such as trails, signage, informational aids, and displays.

The Outdoor Education Accessibility Survey was designed to:

— Assess the architectural accessibility of nature centers and resources in a nature center according to Minnesota State Building Code Chapter 55, or recommendations made by the Minnesota State Council for the Handicapped.

— Report areas to the nature center director not in compliance with the State Code; and to suggest upgrading facilities to the recommended level of accessibility if below the recommendation.

Procedure for Administration

Each nature center was surveyed by a member of the TR-OE Grant Project staff during fall 1986.

Dissemination of Information

TR-OE Grant Project staff and the director of the nature center discussed the results of the survey and recommendations for upgrading the facility to the mandatory or recommended level of accessibility.

OUTDOOR EDUCATION ACCESSIBILITY SURVEY
DECEMBER, 1986*

OUTDOOR EDUCATION FACILITY _____

STREET ADDRESS _____

CITY/STATE _____ ZIP _____

SURVEYOR _____ PHONE: _____

BUILDING OWNER _____

DATE OPENED _____ ☐ NEW CONSTRUCTION ☐ RENOVATED

MAJOR USE AND BRIEF DESCRIPTION _____

_____

*Developed by the Minnesota State Council for the Handicapped, Metro Square, 7th and Robert Streets, Suite 208, St. Paul, MN 55101. Revised in 1985 by Project for Integrated Recreation in the Community (PIRC), Grant # 029FH40011 and in 1986 by Therapeutic Recreation-Outdoor Education Grant Project, # 029FH60046.

INSTRUCTIONS TO THE SURVEYOR

The items in brackets [S] or [c], indicates that it is a specification of the Minnesota State Building Code Chapter 55, or other statutory or regulatory requirement.

The Minnesota State Building Code Chapter 55 establishes minimum requirements of accessibility for all new construction and structural renovation after November 18, 1975.

Even in those instances where it is not a legal requirement, these provisions present a good standard to strive for.

Recommendations of the Minnesota State Council for the Handicapped are also listed.

Surveyors are encouraged to use the comments section to give more detail when there is a discrepancy between the building's current status and the requirement.

PARKING

	Current Status	Requirement	Recommendation
1. How many off-street parking spaces are provided?	_____		
[2.] How many of these parking spaces are provided for use by disabled persons? If none, go to question #7.	_____	1 per 50 or a fraction of 50	
3. What is the surface of the parking area?	_____		Paved
[4.] How many of the handicapped parking spaces are designated with upright, permanent signs?	_____	All must be identified	
[a.] Are the signs visible to a motorist inside a vehicle parked in the space?	_____	Yes	
[b.] Do the signs display the International Symbol of Accessibility?	_____	Yes	
[c.] Are the signs white characters on a blue background?	_____	Yes	
[d.] Do the signs require display of a state certificate or license?	_____	Yes	
[5.] How wide is the space reserved for use by disabled people?	_____	Minimum of 12'	
[6.] Are the handicapped parking spaces located as near as possible to an accessible building entrance?	_____	Yes	

TELEPHONES

	Current Status	Requirement	Recommendation
7. Are phones provided for public use?	_____		
[a.] If yes, what is the height of the highest operable part of the lowest phone?	_____	54" maximum	
[b.] How wide is the space in front of the phone?	_____	30" in width	
[c.] How much room is there in front of the phone?	_____	12" in depth	
d. Does any phone have a volume control for hearing-impaired persons?	_____		Yes, at least one
e. Does any phone have special provisions for persons with hearing aids?	_____		Yes, at least one

WATER FOUNTAINS

	Current Status	Requirement	Recommendation
8. Are water fountains provided?	_____		
[a.] If yes, what is the height of the spout of the lowest mounted water fountain?	_____	33" maximum	
[b.] Describe the type of control and location		Hand-operated up front	

SANITATION FACILITIES

	Current Status	Requirement	Recommendation
9. Are there any toilet facilities? If no, go to #41.			
[10.] If this is an hotel or apartment building, how many guest rooms or dwelling units are equipped for disabled persons?		Refer to Table on page 15	
[11.] How many public toilet facilities are equipped for disabled persons?		Refer below*	
[12.] Are any of these equipped facilities listed in the building directory?		Yes	
[13.] Are the facilities accessible from inside the building without leaving and re-entering?		Yes	
[14.] Is there a continuous route of travel to the bathrooms without steps or abrupt changes in level? If no, describe:		Yes	

*At least one bathroom for each sex must be accessible. If a building has two or more bathrooms for each sex, at least two bathrooms for each sex must be accessible.

PLEASE ANSWER THE FOLLOWING QUESTIONS ABOUT FACILITIES EQUIPPED FOR HANDICAPPED PERSONS. IF THERE AREN'T ANY EQUIPPED FACILITIES USE A TYPICAL FACILITY. GIVE ANSWERS FOR BOTH WOMEN'S AND MEN'S OR UNISEX FACILITIES, WHERE APPLICABLE.

	Women's	Men's or Unisex		
[15.] Is the door or entry identified as accessible?			Yes	By International Symbol of Accessibility
[16.] What is the width of the clear useable opening of the door or doorway (that is, from the face of the door when open at 90° to the face of the opposite door stop)?			31" minimum	34" minimum
[17.] What is the rise of the threshold?			1/2" maximum	

	Current Status		Requirement	Recommendation
	Women's	Men's or Unisex		
118.] What is the height of the door latch hardware from the floor?			42" maximum	
119.] Describe the door latch hardware (e.g., round knob, lever handle, U-shape pull, push plate, etc.).			Lever	
120.] Can the door latch hardware be operated with a single movement of one hand by persons with minimal grip strength?			Yes	
121.] How much room is there next to the latch side of the door so that a person in a wheelchair can approach and open it? (illustration below)			12" minimum	24"
22. Are entry doors equipped with kickplates?				Yes
23. Is the entry through two doors or doorways that form a vestibule or foyer? (illustration below)				
[a.] If yes, what is the depth of the vestibule?			7' minimum	
[b.] What is the clear useable opening of the second door?			31" minimum	34" minimum

Comments:

	Current Status		Requirement	Recommendation
	Women's	Men's or Unisex		
[24.] Is the toilet room floor one common level?			Yes	
25. Is there a place that provides a full five foot diameter clear floor space in the toilet room?			Yes	Yes
[26.] Is there clear knee space under at least one sink for a person in a wheelchair?			Yes	
[a.] If yes, how tall is that space?			29" minimum	30"
[b.] How wide is that space?			31" minimum	
[c.] Not counting the drain pipe, how deep is that space?			12" minimum	
[27.] What is the height of the top of the sink rim from the floor?			34" maximum	
[28.] Specify the faucet hardware (e.g., lever action, round knob, tip-tap, etc.)			Lever	Yes
29. Are drain and waste pipes covered or insulated to prevent burns?				
[30.] What are the working heights from the floor of the following:			40" maximum	
[a.] Soap dispenser control			40" maximum	

Comments:

	Current Status		Requirement	Recommendation
	Women's	Men's or Unisex		
[b.] Towel dispenser control			40" maximum	
[c.] Disposal unit's top edge			40" maximum	
[d.] Mirror's lowest edge			40" maximum	
[e.] Product dispenser control			40" maximum	
[f.] Shelf top			40" maximum	
[g.] Other _____			40" maximum	
31. Are urinals provided?				
[a.] If yes, what is the height from the floor of the top of the lip of the lowest urinal?			18" maximum	
[b.] How wide a space is there to approach the urinal?			31" minimum	
[32.] How much clear floor space is between the front of the toilet bowl and the nearest obstruction (i.e., closed stall door, wall, heat register, etc.)?			36" minimum	
[33.] How wide is the approach area to the accessible toilet?			36" minimum	40"
34. Is the accessible toilet enclosed by privacy screens?				Yes, if more than one toilet

Comments:

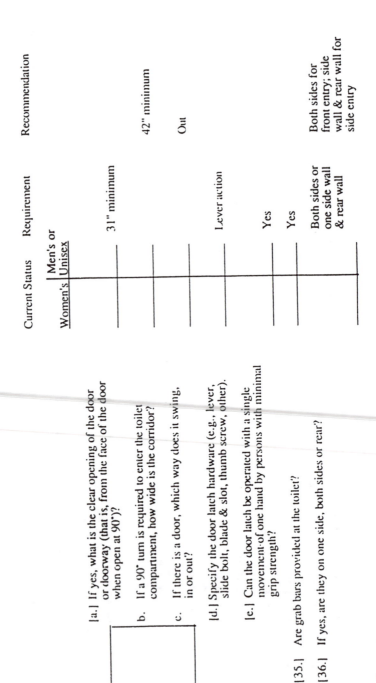

	Current Status		Requirement	Recommendation
	Women's	Men's or Unisex		
[a.] If yes, what is the clear opening of the door or doorway (that is, from the face of the door when open at 90°)?			31" minimum	
b. If a 90° turn is required to enter the toilet compartment, how wide is the corridor?				42" minimum
c. If there is a door, which way does it swing, in or out?				Out
[d.] Specify the door latch hardware (e.g., lever, slide bolt, blade & slot, thumb screw, other).			Lever action	
[e.] Can the door latch be operated with a single movement of one hand by persons with minimal grip strength?			Yes	
[35.] Are grab bars provided at the toilet?			Yes	
[36.] If yes, are they on one side, both sides or rear?			Both sides or one side wall & rear wall	Both sides for front entry; side wall & rear wall for side entry

Comments:

	Current Status		Requirement	Recommendation
	Women's	Men's or Unisex		
[37.] What is the outside diameter of these bars?			1-1/2"	
[38.] What is the clearance from walls or partitions?			1-1/2"	
[39.] On the side wall(s):				
[a.] Is there a horizontal component?			Yes	
[b.] What is the lowest point above the seat?			10"	
[c.] How far does it extend in front of the toilet bowl?			6" minimum	
[d.] How long is the bar?			12" minimum	
[e.] Is there a vertical component?			Yes	
[f.] How far is it mounted from in front of the toilet bowl?			12"	
[g.] How far is it mounted above the toilet seat?			12"	
[h.] How long is the bar?			18"	

Comments:

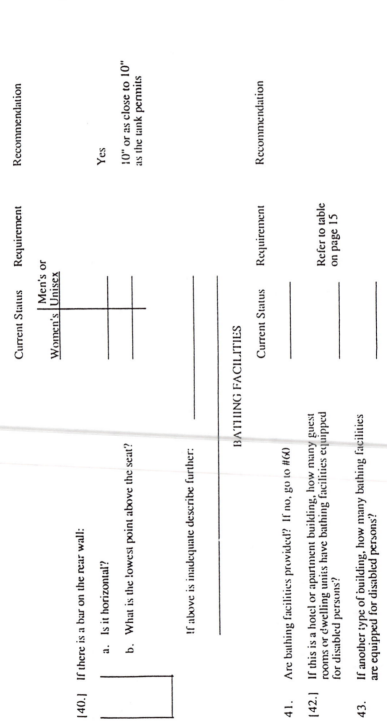

Current Status   Requirement   Recommendation

40.] If there is a bar on the rear wall:

   a. Is it horizontal? — Requirement: Men's or Unisex / Women's — Recommendation: Yes

   b. What is the lowest point above the seat? — Recommendation: 10" or as close to 10" as the tank permits

If above is inadequate describe further:

_____

BATHING FACILITIES

Current Status   Requirement   Recommendation

41. Are bathing facilities provided? If no, go to #60

42.] If this is a hotel or apartment building, how many guest rooms or dwelling units have bathing facilities equipped for disabled persons? — Requirement: Refer to table on page 15

43. If another type of building, how many bathing facilities are equipped for disabled persons?

Comments:

	Current Status	Requirement	Recommendation

44. Is there a door or doorway to the tub room or shower compartment?

 [a.] If yes, what is the clear useable opening (that is, from the face of the door when open at 90° to the face of the opposite door stop)?   _____   31" minimum   34" minimum

 [b.] What is the threshold height?   _____   1/2" maximum

[45.] Is there a fixed, folding or retractable seat available to use in the bathtub or shower? If yes, give dimensions of: _____   Yes

 [a.] Height from floor   _____   17" - 20"

 b. Width   _____   15"   18" minimum

 [c.] Depth   _____

46. Is there a shower?   _____

[47.] Is the shower head hand-held with a flexible hose?   _____   Yes, if no shower is provided

 [a.] If yes, how long is the flexible hose?   _____   6' minimum

 [b.] If there is a vertical height adjustment bar, how long is it?   _____   4' minimum

Comments:

	Current Status	Requirement	Recommendation
[48.] Specify the type of water control valves (e.g., knob, lever action, other).	_____	Lever action	
[49.] Are the controls reachable from the seat?	_____	Yes	
[50.] If there is a tub area, are grab bars provided? If no, go to #55.		Yes	
[51.] What is the outside diameter of these bars?	_____	1-1/2"	
[52.] What is the clearance from the walls?	_____	1-1/2"	
[53.] Is there a horizontal bar?	_____	Yes	
[a.] How high is it above the rim of the tub?	_____	4" - 6"	
[b.] How long is it?	_____	36" minimum	
[54.] Is there a vertical bar?	_____	Yes	
[a.] How far is it mounted from the end of the tub?	_____	30"	
[b.] How high is the bottom of the bar from the rim of the tub?	_____	9"	
[c.] How long is the bar?	_____	42"	

	Current Status	Requirement	Recommendation
[55.] If there is a shower compartment, are grab bars provided?	_____	Yes	
[56.] What is the outside diameter of these bars?	_____	1-1/2"	
[57.] What is the clearance from the walls?	_____	1-1/2"	
[58.] Is there a vertical bar?	_____	Yes	
[a.] On what wall is it mounted, in relation to the seat?	_____	On the wall opposite the seat	
[b.] How high is the bottom of the bar from the floor?	_____	36"	
[c.] How long is the bar?	_____	24"	
[59.] Is there a horizontal bar?	_____	Yes	
[a.] On what wall is it mounted, in relation to the seat?	_____	On the wall adjacent to seat	
[b.] How high is it above the seat?	_____	10"	
[c.] How long is it?	_____	18"	

Comments:

TRAILS

Trail Name	Current Status	Requirement	Recommendation
60. Are the trails continuous, without abrupt changes in level (e.g., ruts, potholes, drainage structure)?	___		Yes
61. What is the texture and degree of compactness of the surface?	___		Firm, Smooth
62. What is the width of the trail?	___		4" minimum for one way travel. 6' min. for two way travel
63. What is the steepest slope of the trail?	___		8.33% maximum
64. Are there drop offs on either side of the trail?	___		Yes - rail, rope minimum
a. If yes, are handrails provided along the trail?	___		32" maximum
b. What is the distance from the rail to the ground?	___		2" maximum
c. What is the circumference gripping surface of the handrail?	___		clear area of 8'6"
65. Is the area above the trail unobstructed? (e.g., branches)	___		4' maximum
66. If there are gates along the trail, how high is the latch from the ground?	___		Hiking only
67. What is the designated use assigned to the trail?	___		Yes, with enough space not to block the path
68. Are teaching stations located off the trail accessible?	___		Yes, surface variations will guide individuals w/ visual impairments
69. Is the trail edge distinguishable?	___		

SIGNAGE, INFORMATIONAL AIDS AND DISPLAYS

	Current Status	Requirement	Recommendation
70. Is the park entry sign clearly marked with the international symbol of access?	_____		Yes
71. Do all informational signage (e.g., trails, interpretive displays, restrooms) consist of large lettering or characters raised or recessed from the background?	_____		Yes
72. What is the distance from the signs to the ground?	_____		24" maximum
73. Are brown and white "permitted use" blanks and "permitted use" decals posted where trail is accessible?	_____		Yes
74. Are pre-recorded messages or other informational aids available for individuals with visual impairments to recognize the trail system or interpret informational displays?	_____		Yes
75. Are sounding boxes, different surface textures, or other devices used to indicate change in the trail direction for persons with visual impairment?	_____		Yes

BENCHES

	Current Status	Requirement	Recommendation
76. Are seating areas located adjacent to main pathways?	_____		Yes
77. Are there any abrupt level changes between pathways and seating areas?	_____		No
78. How much unobstructed space is available adjacent to the benches?	_____		5' minimum
79. Do benches and chairs have back rests and arm supports?	_____		Yes
80. Is there a clear area on either end of the bench for a wheelchair or stroller?	_____		Yes-30" minimum
81. How deep are the seats?	_____		18"
82. What is the height of the bench seat from the ground?	_____		18"
83. What is the distance between the trail and the seating area?	_____		24" minimum
84. What materials are the benches constructed of?	_____		Non-abrasive, non-splintering material that does not retain heat or cold

TRASH CANS/RECEPTACLES

85. Are trash receptacles located adjacent to but not obstructing trails and pathways? _____ Yes

86. What is the distance from the ground to the trash can opening? _____ 36"

87. Can opening be used with a single arm motion? _____ Yes

88. Describe the surfaces and edges of the trash receptacles. _____ smooth and rounded

SPECTATOR AREA/AMPHITHEATRE

	Current Status	Requirement	Recommendation
89. Is there a pathway adjacent to spectator area?	_____		Yes
90. What is the surface of the pathway?	_____		firm, level, smooth
91. Is there an inclined path leading to spectator area? (If not, go to question #92)			
a. What is the slope of this path?	_____		8.33% maximum
b. Is a handrail provided?	_____		Yes
c. What is the distance from the ground to the handrail?	_____		32" maximum
d. Does the handrail extend an additional 2' at the top and the bottom of the incline?	_____		Yes
92. How wide are the aisles in the spectator area?	_____		4'
93. Is accessible seating provided in a variety of areas?	_____		Yes
94. Are railings and wheelstops provided in front of accessible spectator seating area?	_____		Yes
95. How high are railings from ground?	_____		Ideal 3' maximum

DOCKS

	Current Status	Requirement	Recommendation
96. How wide is walkway leading to the docks?	___		5" wide
97. Is there an incline in adjacent walkway leading to docks? (If not, go to #98)			
a. What is the slope of the walkway?	___		8.33% maximum
b. Are handrails provided?	___		Yes
c. What is the distance between the ground and the handrails?	___		32" maximum
d. What is the diameter of the handrail grip?	___		2" maximum
98. What is the surface of the dock?	___		non-slip with spacings on dock less than 1/2"
99. Is the fishing dock equipped with railings?	___		Yes
100. What is the height of the railing?	___		36" maximum
101. Are 4" kickplates placed along the dock edge?	___		Yes, for safety purposes
102. Is the surface of the boat dock level with boats used in this facility?	___		Yes, generally

BEACHES

	Current Status	Requirement	Recommendation
103. Is there a continuous pathway from parking lot to bath house to swimming beach?	_____		Yes
104. What is the surface of this path?	_____		non-skid, concrete asphalt, wood plank
105. Is this an inclined path?	_____		
106. What is the maximum slope of this pathway?	_____		8.33% minimum
107. Are handrails available alongside the path?	_____		Yes
108. What is the distance between the ground and the handrail?	_____		32"
109. What is the diameter of the handrail grip?	_____		2"
110. Is there a level area in the water at the bottom of this path?	_____		Yes
111. Describe the surface material.	_____		6' - 6' pad
112. Is the floor of the swimming area level without abrupt changes or dropoffs?	_____		Yes
113. What is the maximum slope?	_____	8.33% maximum	

Appendix D

Resources for Information: Agencies and Associations Serving Persons with Disabilities

Access Alaska
3550 Airport Wy., #3
Fairbanks, AK 99701

Activities Unlimited, Inc.
P. O. Box 324
Helena, MT 59624

Alternative Mobility
Adventure Seekers
Boise State University
Physical Education Dept.
1910 University Drive
Boise, ID 83725

American Foundation for the
Blind, Inc.
15 West 16th Street
New York, NY 10011

Arc of the United States
2501 Avenue J
Arlington, TX 76006

Association for Children and
Adults with Learning Disabilities
4156 Library Road
Pittsburgh, PA 15234

Association of
Experiential Education
C.U. Box 249
Boulder, CO 80309

Bradford Woods Outdoor
Education Center
5040 State Road 67 North
Martinsville, IN 46151

Breckenridge Outdoor
Education Center
P.O. Box 697
Breckenridge, CO 80424

Challenge Alaska
P.O. Box 110065
Anchorage, AK 99511

Council for Exceptional Children
1920 Association Drive
Reston, VA 22091

CW Hog
Box 8118
Pocatello, ID 83209

Environmental Travel
Companions
Fort Mason Center, Building C
San Francisco, CA 94123

Epilepsy Foundation of America
4351 Garden City Drive
Suite 406
Landover, MD 20785

Information   Center   for
Individuals with Disabilities
20 Providence St.
Room 329
Boston, MA 02116

Muscular Dystrophy Association
810 7th Avenue
New York, NY 10019

National Amputation
Foundation
12-45 150th Street
Whitestone, NY 11357

National Association for
Mental Health
10 Columbus Circle
New York, NY 10019

National Association of Developmental Disabilities Council
1234 Massachusetts Avenue N.W.
Suite 103
Washington, D.C. 20005

National Association
of Interpretation
P. O. Box 1892
Fort Collins, CO 80522

National Association of the Deaf
814 Thayer Avenue
Silver Springs, MD 20910

National Down Syndrome Society
141 5th Avenue
New York, NY 10010

National Easter Seal Society
2023 W. Ogden Avenue
Chicago, IL 60612

National Federation of the Blind
1800 Johnson Street
Baltimore, MD 21230

National Handicapped Sports
4405 East-West Highway #603
Bethesda, MD 20814

National Head Injury Foundation
280 Singletary Lane
Framingham, MA 01701

National Information Center
on Deafness
Gallaudet College Kendall Green
Washington, D.C. 20003

National Multiple
Sclerosis Society
205 E. 42nd Street
New York, NY 10017

National Paraplegia Fundation
333 North Michigan Avenue
Chicago, IL 60601

National Society of
Autistic Children
1234 Massachusetts Avenue N.W.
Suite 1017
Washington, D.C. 20005

National Spinal Cord Injury
Foundation
369 Elliot Street
Newton Upper Falls, MA 02164

National Therapeutic Recreation
Society/National Recreation and
Park Association
3101 Park Center Drive
Alexandria, VA 22302

Outward Bound
690 Market St. #500
San Francisco, CA 94101

Paraplegics on Independent
Nature Trips (POINT)
3200 Mustang Drive
Grapevine, TX 76051

Shared Outdoor Adventure
Recreation (SOAR)
P.O. Box 14583
Portland, OR 14583

The Association for Persons with
Severe Handicaps
11201 Greenwood Ave. N.
Seattle, WA 98133

United Cerebral Palsy Association
66 East 34th Street
New York, NY 10016

Wilderness Inquiry
1313 5th Street S.E.
Minneapolis, MN 55414

Appendix E

Participant Screening:
Supplemental Participant Information

WI Interviewer:_____ Date:_____

Spoke to:_____Title:_____Relationship:_____

HEALTH AND ABILITIES

Type(s) of disability:_____

_____

_____

_____

Wheelchair (type):_____ Crutches:_____ Cane:_____

Weight:_____ Height:_____ Age:_____ Smoker_____ Physician:_____

Current Health Status:_____

Paddling ability:_____

Camping experience:_____

Type of trip they are looking for:_____

Balance:_____ Strength:_____

Seizures   Type:_____ Frequency:_____

Duration:_____ Time last seizure occurred:_____

Describe:_____

_____

Do they have an aura:_____ Describe:_____

_____

Swimming Ability: Afraid of water___Cannot swim___Can float___50 yards___Can swim well___

PFD needed: Class 1 _____ Class 5 _____ Class 3 _____

Communications needs (interpreter, talk board, pencil & paper):_____

Degree of independence or assistance with ADL's

Is help needed: Eating:_____ Toileting:_____ Dressing:_____ Attendant used?:_____

_____

Bowel & Bladder Program:_____

Allergies, describe reaction:_____

_____

Dietary needs:_____

Will they bring any special food of their own?_____

If yes, what and how much?_____

SOCIAL APPROPRIATENESS AND NEEDS

Describe problem behavior:_____

_____

_____

_____

Recommended intervention (include who recommended it):

_____

_____

SPECIAL EQUIPMENT NEEDS

Wheelchair (what kind)?_____   Foldable _____

Other ambulatory aids?_____   Toileting aids:_____

Other aids?_____   Straws, remained to bring:_____

WI EQUIPMENT NEEDS

Thermarest_____   Sleeping Bag_____
Camprest_____   Wool Shirt (Size)_____
One arm paddle_____   Wool Pants (Size)_____
Coleman Seat_____   Rain Gear_____
Sling Seat_____   Helmet_____
Additional Padding_____   Class One PFD_____
Flexion Mitts_____   Lawn Chair(only if they have sensation)_____

OTHER INFORMATION

Transportaion needs:_____

Other:_____

_____

_____

_____

_____

Appendix F

If You Have a Mobility Impairment

If you normally use crutches to get around, you should be able to get around independently 99.9 percent of the time. If you use a wheelchair, you will be probably be able to cross some of the trails, but you are likely to require help along the way. Much depends on your level of muscle function and the nature of the trail, but many agencies successfully integrate people who use wheelchairs on every trip they take, often including people who are functionally quadriplegic from a spinal cord injury, cerebral palsy, or some other condition. Although that may sound odd to some, it is really not a big deal. After a while, the wheelchairs always seem to fade into the background. If you are accepted into the program, you will get the assistance you need to have a safe and enjoyable trip.

If you need occasional assistance on the trail, such as transferring to and from canoes and tents, or crossing portages, the staff will provide you with the assistance you need. In most cases, the only restriction is weight (and that depends on the trip). If you use a wheelchair and weigh more than 160 pounds, your choice of trips may be limited to rivers, sea kayaking, or in the winter, dog sledding.

If you need assistance with eating, dressing, toileting, and other personal hygiene issues, a personal care attendant is required. If you have an attendant that would like to go on the trip, please send the application to the agency when you apply. Agencies also have people who are willing to serve as attendants if you do not know one. You are financially responsible for the attendant's trip fees. Financial aid is available if necessary, however. Please request a financial aid application form if you need financial help. Sign language interpreters are also provided for participants who need them.

Many people are concerned with toileting issues in the wilderness. Don't be. Agencies bring a portable commode that provides plenty of comfort and stability. They also make an effort to ensure privacy and cleanliness. Don't be concerned if your bathroom routines require extra time or a regular schedule—you'll have the time you need. In addition to the commode, other adaptations for canoe seating, paddling with one arm, sleeping on the ground, *etc.*, are available—accommodations that truly help everyone enjoy and participate in the trip to the full extent of their ability.

INDEX